WHAT PEOPLE ARE SAYING ABOUT THIS BOOK

"Chad Lewis is THE authority on things that 'go bump in the night.' We just hope that he won't have us turned into newts by a goblin or something."

—Mike McKay & Donuts
Wisconsin Radio Morning Show *Hot Country B-95*

"Chad Lewis, master of Wisconsin macabre and prowler of the globe in his search for the unexplained, has now proven himself equally adept at time travel. In his new book, Lewis pulls readers along on a hell-bent journey through the state's historic newspaper record of weird and grisly events. Lewis provides both a fascinating read and a valuable resource in this one volume, and shows that the good old days were also the weird old days."

—Linda Godfrey
Author of *Weird Michigan, The Beast of Bray Road, Hunting the American Werewolf, The Poison Widow,* and co-author of *Weird Wisconsin*

"A colorful walk through Wisconsin history allowing the observant reader a window to the past. Let Mr. Lewis' research entertain, scare and inform your every sense. Destined to be found in the bibliographies of every industry book from here on!"

—Noah Voss
Paranormal investigator, author of *UFO Wisconsin*
UFOwisconsin.com, GetGhostGear.com

HIDDEN HEADLINES
OF
WISCONSIN

Strange, Unusual, & Bizarre Newspaper Stories
1860-1910

Researched and Compiled by
Chad Lewis

Foreword by Michael Bie

UNEXPLAINED
Research Publishing Company
A Division of Unexplained Research, LLC

Library of Congress Control Number: 2007921941
ISBN-13: 978-0-9762099-6-6
ISBN-10: 0-9762099-6-9

Printed in the United States by Documation

Unexplained Research Publishing Company
A Division of Unexplained Research LLC
P.O. Box 2173, Eau Claire, WI 54702-2173
Email: info@unexplainedresearch.com
www.unexplainedresearch.com

Cover Design: Jeannine & Terry Fisk
Illustrations: Rick Fisk
Portrait: Rob Mattison

DEDICATION

This book is dedicated to the people of Wisconsin who lived through the strange, unusual, and bizarre.

TABLE OF CONTENTS

FOREWORD

Isn't it fun to relive the good old days when the only trials and tribulations in life were getting locked in the root cellar or saving enough pennies to buy a new plow horse—just like what happened to Ma and Pa and Laura and Half-Pint on *Little House on the Prairie*?

Nah.

You know as well as I do the "good old days" were anything but that. Not with insanity, premature burials, and spontaneous human combustion running rampant across the land...and those are just a few of the things detailed in this fascinating new book from Chad Lewis.

Maybe it's our natural tendency to inject sepia-toned nostalgia into days long gone, maybe it's because modern culture so often gives us sanitized versions of our past (*Little House* will run indefinitely on cable), but scratch below the surface and you'll find that our forefathers' common experience was far more incredible than anything we can imagine today. That's what makes *Hidden Headlines of Wisconsin* such a compelling and valuable read.

Hidden Headlines of Wisconsin dishes up true accounts of the past without the filter, and the truth is...things were downright bizarre. How else can you describe men behaving like dogs and shoes made of human flesh; lightening-induced insanity or frightfully accurate premonitions of death?

Chad Lewis has done us a tremendous service by mining news accounts from the early 1900s to provide this compelling collection of the strange and mysterious. Chad knows his way around the subject—his research into unexplained phenomena has taken him around the world. We're lucky he has chosen the Badger State for his latest endeavor.

Hidden Headlines of Wisconsin deserves a place in your library alongside *Wisconsin Death Trip*, the groundbreaking 1973 book that revealed an eye-opening glimpse of the human condition in Black River Falls, Wis., circa late 19th century. *Hidden Headlines of Wisconsin* provides no less of a stunning portrait, and it's indispensable for presenting the past as it truly happened...amnesiacs, ghosts, man-beasts and all.

Michael Bie
Classic Wisconsin
www.classicwisconsin.com

Introduction

In today's often hectic world you hear people longing for a simpler time. To many, the past represents a slower pace of life when crime, stress, and drugs, were thought to be non-existent. I too long for that past, I long for a time when you could step out of your country home and take a leisurely stroll down past the local pharmacy to the city pond where kids would be fishing the day away right next to where the sea serpent was spotted. It was a time when courting sweethearts could go for a quiet drive through the countryside and be terrorized by the "wild man." It was a time when family was still important in our lives and loving parents proudly gave birth to a half dog and half child. It was a time when starry eyed kids gazed into the dark night sky and wondered about the universe while watching a hovering disk slowly float over their home.

Unfortunately, the past is simply the past, and no wishing will ever bring it back. Yet these stories provide a rare opportunity to vicariously experience what it is was like to be a resident living in early Wisconsin. Allow yourself to be transported back to a time long since past, but be prepared, the newspapers of old were not quite like those of today. The style of writing, along with the spattering of aged words may appear a bit old fashioned and archaic to you, but if you let it this "old" type of writing will make you feel like you heard the stories straight off the lips of the town gossip. Also remember that the papers of this time were certainly not politically correct. If Old Man Olson blew his brains out with a shotgun, that is actually what the paper reported, complete with all the grizzly details. The papers also tended to cover a story in a manner that often left the reader with many unanswered questions. What ever happened to the chicken with a human face? Was that town haunting ever solved? Did the residents ever find the mysterious object that crashed into the ground? These and many more questions are left for you to speculate on, or perhaps even solve.

Of course, as a modern reader with a current perspective you may undoubtedly look at these cases and wonder if someone listed as "dying of fright" actually died of a heart attack while they were frightened. You may also wonder whether that "wild man" with long black body hair that was spotted roaming the woods was actually a Bigfoot, or that just maybe that "hovering meteor" was really a UFO. However, as you will see I have not made any judgment as to the validity of these cases or I have also refrained from telling you whether or not I even believe them, I have simply presented them to you as exactly the way you would have read them on the day they were printed.

Regardless of what conclusions you come to after reading this book I am certain that these Wisconsin stories will provide you a glimpse of the state in its simpler, slower-paced, and much much weirder past.

Enjoy the adventure,
Chad Lewis

ACKNOWLEDGMENTS

I would like to thank Nisa Giaquinto, Sarah Szymanski, Douglas Connell, Rob Mattison, Rick Fisk, Jeannine Fisk, and Terry Fisk for assisting with the research and production of this book.

Girl Dies Of Broken Heart After Pet Chicken Is Killed

LA CROSSE- In the spring of 1861, when the calls to patriotism went like wildfire over the land, a young man in the Third Ward of this city, named George Treyser, was engaged to be married to a young lady here. He enlisted and promised to return as soon as the war was over, leaving his fiancée almost brokenhearted.

Treyser was killed at the Battle of Wilson Creek and when the sad news reached La Crosse his betrothed went into fainting fits and for two days her life was despaired of. She never recovered her reason entirely and lived under a shadow of impenetrable gloom. She soon selected a chicken from a brood and took it to her room where she made a pet of it. She gave it a name which, in time, it knew and soon came at her call. It would perch on her head as she sat looking out her window, and pock crumbs from her lips when she was fit to feed it, and pick at her teeth as though they were kernels of corn.

She would sit for hours caressing the chicken, which grew into a sleek and pretty rooster as ever lived, and which formed an affection for its mistress truly wonderful. And thus the pair lived until three weeks ago when the chicken was killed by a dog. Since that time the girl grew languid, nervous, and disheartened, and finally last week she died with a broken heart.

Such, in brief, is an actual incident which thus passes into the history of the singular freaks of affection. Had their earnest vows ever been consummated, it is no hazard to say the lives of the gallant soldier and his loving choice would have been happy, as hand in hand they walked the dark aisles of care and earth's troubles.

—La Crosse Democrat
August 22, 1864

❖ ❖ ❖

Janesville Woman Killed By Grief
Mrs. David Acheson, Whose Daughter Was Burned To Death, Passes Away

JANESVILLE- Mrs. David Acheson of the town of Magnolia died suddenly last night from the shock caused by the tragic death of her 13-year-old daughter, who was accidentally burned to death this week.

—Milwaukee Journal
January 11, 1899

❖ ❖ ❖

Woman May Have Been Buried Alive

WEST SUPERIOR- Relatives of Mrs. A.S. Wilfoung, who is supposed to have died Wednesday night and buried early Thursday morning think the woman was not dead when she was buried, as a few hours before the interment was made she showed signs of animation. Doctors who were in attendance, however, pronounced her dead and the services were held. The woman was in a trance for fifteen hours before she was declared dead, and it is feared by some she was in a trance when she was buried. A brother of the dead woman went at once to Duluth, where the interment was made, to have the grave opened, and ascertain whether life was extinct before his sister was buried.

—Milwaukee Journal
January 13, 1899

> **The fear of being buried alive was so prevalent that devices were invented and patented to insure a safe burial. One strange device was a spring-loaded casket lid that could be opened by the slightest movement from inside the coffin.**

Toper Drinks Water And Then Dies
John Moss Of La Crosse Dies After Imbibing A Glass Of Well Water

LA CROSSE- After drinking heavily for two weeks, John Moss, an ex-convict, died just after he had drank a glass of cold water. Moss went out to a well in the rear of the saloon and pumped and drank a glass of water. He returned to the saloon, sat down in a chair and died five minutes afterward, without making the slightest kind of struggle or move of his body. He was 49 years old and came to this city from Dubuque, where he has relatives. About a year ago he was sent to Waupun for one year for breaking in and stealing chickens from the county poor farm.

—*Milwaukee Journal*
January 12, 1900

❖❖❖

Fear Their Child
Was Buried Alive

**Mr. And Mrs. Charles Behrens Ask
To Have The Body Exhumed.
Physician Certified To The Death Of
4-Year-Old Daughter.
Other Children Apparently Dead
Were Afterward Resuscitated.**

MILWAUKEE- Mr. and Mrs. Charles Behrens, 873 Sixth Street, fear that their little child, Mary, aged 4 years, was buried alive in the Calvary Cemetery, Nov. 18, and have asked permission of the heath department to disinter the remains and satisfy themselves whether or not such was the case. The child was taken ill of scarlet fever and became unconscious and for two days laid in the home like one dead. The attending physician certified to its death and the funeral was held. The mother was ill at the time and did not see the baby before it was carried to its grave.

Other children of the family became ill and the parents changed physicians in the hope of better results. One of the children lay unconscious for a long time, but was resuscitated, and it is this fact that leads the par-

ents to the apprehension that the other child was not really dead. The child had been ill but one day before it lapsed into the death-like stupor.

The health authorities do not believe that the child was alive when buried but in order to allay the fears of the parents a disinterment will be allowed if the request is insisted upon. Registrar Coon of the health department referred Mr. Behrens to Dr. Grosskoph, who has charge of the Calvary Cemetery. Dr. Grosskopf said this afternoon that no request had been made to him, but that he would allow the disinterment if desired in order to relieve the parental anxiety.

—*Milwaukee Journal*
January 13, 1900

Another safety precaution against being buried alive was called the cemetery bell. This bell sat on top of the grave with a rope going down to the "deceased." If someone awoke in their coffin they could simply pull the cord to alert the caretaker.

CHAPTER 1 BIZARRE DEATHS

Cried Herself To Death

NEENAH- Elsie Whetsan, aged 4, died here yesterday. The baby's mother passed away last Friday and she cried herself to death.

—*Milwaukee Journal*
May 29, 1900

The town of Cartwright has been renamed as New Auburn.

Panther Devours A Little Girl

CARTWRIGHT- An 8-year-old daughter of C.F. Riley, a farmer living sixteen miles from here in the Mad Brook settlement, has been carried away by a panther and devoured. Only a few fragments of the remains could be found. The girl was walking in the road near the farm when the beast sprang from the woods, and taking the girl in his huge jaws, carried her into a swamp where she was torn limb-from-limb. The few scattered remains were gathered up and buried.

The community has organized in a panther hunt, and the farmers will not lay aside their guns until the brutes are exterminated. Since they started out a panther measuring 10 feet has been shot and two others have been seen.

—*Milwaukee Journal*
December 4, 1900

According to the Wisconsin Department of Natural Resources, panthers no longer call Wisconsin home, although even today people claim to see them roaming the state.

Fright Kills Young Woman

BELOIT- A young woman named Smith, employed as domestic at Footville, was so frightened as she came out of a store by two men who were racing horses up the street that she fell dead. Her home was at Richland Center and she was 25 years of age.

—*Milwaukee Journal*
January 17, 1901

Architect Frank Lloyd Wright was born in Richland Center in 1867.

HIDDEN HEADLINES of WISCONSIN

Dies On His Way Home From Wife's Funeral
Old Resident Of Stoddard, Wis., Loses His Way In The Woods And Dies From Exhaustion

LA CROSSE- To become fatigued and die on the way home from his wife's funeral, is the peculiar fate of John Jonas, an aged resident of Stoddard, Wis. Saturday word was brought to that village stating that the old man whose age was 78 years, had turned up missing and no trace could be found of him. The last seen of him was at the funeral of his second wife, with whom he was not living. He left for home after attending the funeral services and was not seen alive afterward. A search was instituted immediately for the old man and the party came upon the remains about a mile from his home. He had evidently become lost in the woods and not having any food, and not being able to locate the road, fell down from sheer exhaustion, and perished. The remains were taken to town and buried. The body had apparently only lain on the ground a day or so.

—*Milwaukee Journal*
December 21, 1900

Frightened To Death
Five-year-Old Boy Mistakes Two Hogs For Black Bears

MADISON- The 5-year-old son of Herman Kohlhepp of Unity was frightened to death Tuesday. The child was playing near the house when two black hogs, which the boy no doubt mistook for bears, gave him such a fright that he died a few hours later from the effects.

—*Milwaukee Journal*
February 28, 1901

❖ ❖ ❖

He Predicted His Own Death
Kenosha Man Made Arrangements To Settle Debts And Then Quietly Waited For Death

KENOSHA- Charles Van Gasbeck died suddenly Sunday afternoon, aged 38 years. He and "Eddie" Griffin were intimate friends, and both had talked about which of the two would be the first to die. Last Saturday they met and Griffin remarked how ill Van Gasbeck was looking, to which the latter answered: "I shall live to see you die, Eddie." Griffin met with a sudden death Saturday night by falling down a flight of stairs and fractured his skull. When Van Gasbeck learned of Griffin's death Sunday morning he was visibly affected and told his wife that he had a presentment that death was approaching, and that he would be a dead man before evening. In spite of her efforts to cheer him he remained despondent. He made arrangements to settle a few small debts, and disposed of property with the firm conviction that he was doomed. When the first hemorrhage began he collapsed entirely.

—*Milwaukee Journal*
February 28, 1901

> **The word presentment was a popular way to explain what we would today label a premonition.**

Laughs At Story And Dies As A Result

KENOSHA- Hollis Lane died suddenly last night. Lane had been chatting and joking with a party a friends for a half hour. A friend had been telling a funny story and Lane seemed to lean ever on his hand as if to laugh the harder. After a minute it was noticed that Lane was leaning against the story-teller, and he was found to be dead.

—*Milwaukee Journal*
March 1, 1901

❖ ❖ ❖

Go Together To Grave
Husband And Wife Die Suddenly On The Same Day

FALL CITY- Mr. and Mrs. Hathaway, old residents of Fall City, died very suddenly

yesterday. Mr. Hathaway died at 2 o'clock a.m. and his wife passed away at 11:30 p.m. The burial will take place next Thursday afternoon.

—*Eau Claire Weekly*
May 2, 1901

❖ ❖ ❖

Twins Die Suddenly
Janesville Children Expire Within Two Hours

JANESVILLE- The twin daughters of Mr. and Mrs. Carl T. Williams of this city died in spasms Saturday within two hours of each other. They were ten days old, weighed seven and one-half pounds each, and had been well until two days ago.

—*Milwaukee Journal*
May 6, 1901

Strange Accident
Simon Brazek, Saved From Asphyxiation, Falls Downs Stairs And Is Killed

INDEPENDENCE- Simon Brazek, a farmer at Independence, went into a smokehouse and fell asleep. Live coals were still in the house and he was taken to the house of a neighbor and resuscitated. He thought he was well enough to walk about, and, arising from bed, attempted to come down-stairs. He fell headlong down the stairs, sustaining injuries from which he died a few moments later.

—*Milwaukee Journal*
October 28, 1901

HIDDEN HEADLINES of WISCONSIN

Wife Dies Of Shock
Officers Falk Loses Daughter And Helpmeet In One Day

MILWAUKEE- Bereft of child and wife in one day, such was the extreme misfortune of officer Edward Falk, 528 Fourth Avenue. The sad duty of attending to the burial of his little 2-year old child Eleanor was being performed Tuesday afternoon by Mr. Falk alone, his wife being sick and could not attend the funeral. That sorrows never come singly, was demonstrated, for upon the return of the bereaved parent, he discovered that his wife had died during his absence. The nervous strain at the loss of her only child had proved fatal. Mr. Falk was crushed by his double loss.

—*Milwaukee Journal*
May 16, 1901

CHAPTER 1 BIZARRE DEATHS

Stricken In Cemetery
Mrs. Augusta Nahf Dies While Visiting Grave Of Daughter

MILWAUKEE- Mrs. Augusta Nahf, 2720 Brown Street, went with a neighbor to visit the grave of another child at Union Cemetery Saturday afternoon, and intended to go from there to Forest Home, where her husband, the late Frederick C. Nahf, is buried. As they were walking through the cemetery Mrs. Nahf sank on a bench beside the in a fainting spell. Medical aid was summoned and she was taken home in a carriage, but was dead when the house was reached. Heart disease was the cause. Mrs. Nahf was 71 years old. The funeral will be held at 2 o'clock Tuesday from the residence to Forest Home Cemetery, the Rev. A. A. Kiehle officiating.

—Milwaukee Journal
June 10, 1901

❖ ❖ ❖

Killed While Returning From Grave Of His Wife

MILWAUKEE- Peter Gergen, aged 81 years, was struck by a Northwestern train at the Eighth Avenue crossing yesterday afternoon, and was instantly killed. Gergen was on the way to the cemetery to visit the grave of his wife. Flagman Williams warned the old man that the train was coming, but Gergen appeared not to hear him. Gergen lived at 483 Twelfth Street and is survived by eight children.

—Milwaukee Journal
September 21, 1901

Knew of Death
Conductor Evans Had Presentiment Of His Fate

RACINE- Evan L. Evans, the conductor who was killed on the Milwaukee Road Saturday, seemed to have a premonition of death, according to a note found in the man's pocket shortly after his body was found. The note read: "If anything should happen to me, I want to be buried in Racine, Wis."

—Milwaukee Journal
October 9, 1901

Breaks Blood Vessel By Cough

LA CROSSE- Grover Downs, aged 17 years, broke a blood vessel during a fit of coughing. He died soon afterward.

—Milwaukee Journal
January 10, 1902

❖ ❖ ❖

Couple Die Together
Mr. And Mrs. Cornelius Vanderwarf Pass Away Within Few Minutes Of Each Other

MILWAUKEE- Death stalked into the household of Cornelius Vanderwarf, 293 Farwell Avenue, Saturday night, and summoned the aged couple within a few moments of each other. Mr. and Mrs. Cornelius Vanderwarf both became ill a few weeks ago, the former having had consumption in a light form for a long time, but on Dec. 19 he took a severe cold, which later developed into pneumonia, and his case became critical.

His faithful wife nursed him up to about a week ago, through an invalid herself, being subject to apoplexy, when she too broke down and sank to the floor in an apoplectic stupor. Being carried to her bed she continued unconscious and Miss Cobb, a trained nurse was called to attend the patients.

Saturday night, shortly after 10 o'clock, Mrs. Vanderwarf breathed her last, although her physician, Dr. Sherman, did not look for a change for the worse so soon. In the meantime, Mr. Vanderwarf, finding it easier to breathe in a sitting position, was half reclining in his armchair within a few feet of his wife's room. The nurse did not deem it wise to tell him of the death of Mrs. Vanderwarf and he, wholly unconscious of her demise, sat in his chair painfully struggling for breath. A few moments after the wife had breathed her last, Miss Cobb heard him arise and start for the room of his wife which he had almost reached when he fell to the floor. She rushed to his side only to find that he too had passed away. Dr. Sherman was hastily summoned and, finding that nothing could be done, went to the invalid son, Allen, who was resting in a wheelchair in an adjoining room, to whom he broke the sad news of the death of both of his parents.

Cornelius Vanderwarf was about 66 years of age and had been a resident of Wisconsin for forty-five years. As a young man, he took a position with the firm

Bradley & Metcalf, and later, becoming a traveling salesman for the firm with southern Wisconsin as a territory, took up the residence at Mazomanie, where he lived for about twenty years. Retiring from business about twelve years ago, he returned to Milwaukee and purchased the present homestead on Farwell Avenue. In 1894 he formed a partnership with Joseph H. Koelsch, purchasing the retail business of the Bradley & Metcalf company, which subsequently was known as the Kenny Shoe company, in which Mr. Vanderwarf retained an interest.

They are survived by one son, Allen, 33 years of age, who has been an invalid from birth and an adopted daughter, Miss Ada Vanderwarf, who resides in Cleveland. A strange coincidence of the death of the aged people within a few moments of each other, was the fact that they had always wished to die together. They have ever been very devoted and dependent upon one another, and Mr. Vanderwarf had been heard to say that when the time came, he hoped that both might go so that there would be no suffering for the survivor.

—*Milwaukee Journal*
December 30, 1901

❖ ❖ ❖

Said She Would Die
Young Girl At Kenosha Predicts Her Demise

KENOSHA- Miss Anna Ziesemer, aged 15, daughter of Mr. and Mrs. John Ziesemer, died Monday of acute peritonitis. Miss Ziesemer was employed at the

Chicago- Rockford hosiery factory. While on the way to her work she chatted pleasantly with her girl companions, but suddenly, when near the factory, turned to one of them and remarked: "I am going to die today." A short distance further she suddenly fell in a faint. She died at her home a few hours later.

—*Milwaukee Journal*
January 29, 1902

❖ ❖ ❖

Death From Tablet
Madison Girl Takes Headache Potion Thought To Have Caused Death

MADISON- Little 7-year-old Eleanor Ryan is dead, supposedly from the effects of a headache tablet. Sunday evening she complained of severe pains in the head, and the tablet was administered. The next morning she was in a comatose state, and died Monday night.

—*Milwaukee Journal*
January 30, 1902

❖ ❖ ❖

Ate Colored Eggs
Died From Poisoning

MARINETTE- Albert Bauer, aged 5, died of ptomaine poisoning, the result of eating colored Easter eggs.

—*Milwaukee Journal*
April 5, 1902

Insured For $1,000
Dies In Two Hours

WAUSAU- Probably the shortest membership ever held in a lodge was that of Abie Nelson of this city in the United Order of Foresters. His policy became effective at midnight, and at 2 o'clock he died of pneumonia. He carried $1,000 insurance.

—*Milwaukee Journal*
May 9, 1902

> **Wausau is the Ginseng capital of the World.**

Fears Come True
Mother Predicted
Tragic Death Of Son
Beloit Brakeman Killed While Coupling Cars. His Head Crushed Between Drawbars. Dictated Pathetic Telegram To His Mother, Telling Her That What She Feared Had Come To Pass.

BELOIT- Frank Van Alstine of this city, a brakeman on the Milwaukee Road, in making a coupling had his head crushed between the drawbars. He lived but a short time. The young man's mother has always been averse to his engaging in railroad worked and feared he would be injured. Before his death, he dictated the following telegram to hcr, "Mother, what you have feared has come to pass. I have been hurt."

—*Milwaukee Journal*
July 4, 1902

Portage Woman Dies From Hardening Of Skin

PORTAGE- Death came to Mrs. Helen M. Richmond from a disease known to the medical profession as schleroderma, or hardening of the skin. She had been affected about three years.

—Milwaukee Journal
July 16, 1902

❖ ❖ ❖

Died From Apoplexy In A Fit of Anger

BELOIT- In a fit of anger over the ruin of her flower garden by a drove of horses, Mrs. Gilbert Halverson was stricken with apoplexy and died yesterday. Her father, Carl A. Cole, once owned a farm in the heart of Milwaukee, a part of which is the site of Juneau Park.

—Milwaukee Journal
August 8, 1902

❖ ❖ ❖

Foretold His Death

MILWAUKEE- Charles Rysticker was found dead on the premises of a quarantined sick man whom he was guarding. He had threatened to quit, saying he was afraid of his life. The indications are that he died in great agony.

—Milwaukee Journal
July 2, 1902

Children Die On Same Day
Farmington Girl, Bitten By Mad Dog, And Her Little Sister Are Buried Together

FARMINGTON- The 16-year-old daughter of Aubert Neumann, town of Farmington, former county treasurer of Polk County, died of lockjaw, caused by the bite of a dog. The girl was bitten about a week ago.

—Eau Claire Leader
September 16, 1910

Shot With Toy Cannon And Dies This Morning

GREEN BAY- John Trich, the 16-year-old-boy who was shot in the abdomen by a bullet from a toy cannon, died this morning.

—Milwaukee Journal
June 27, 1902

❖ ❖ ❖

Jumps Rope 100 Times
Dies Within An Hour

LA CROSSE- Gretchen Henschel, aged 8 years, died here yesterday as the result of jumping rope. She jumped 100 times in succession, then went into the house and became suddenly ill. Death resulted in an hour.

—Milwaukee Journal
April 21, 1902

Woman Dies At A Funeral
Death Of Life-Long Neighbor Overcame Mrs. Maier.
Fatty Degeneration Of The Heart Caused Death.
Attends The Funeral Of Frank Ullrich And Dies In Her Carriage On The Way Back To The City.
An Old Resident.

MILWAUKEE- Mrs. Catherine Maier, aged 63 years, died suddenly yesterday morning while attending the funeral of Frank Ullrich, a life-long friend, at Calvary Cemetery. Death is said to have been caused by fatty degeneration of the heart and the excitement due to the death of Mr. Ullrich. Mrs. Maier lived at 1119 Cherry Street, where she had made her home for neatly forty years, and during nearly all this time had lived next door to Mr. Ullrich, and his death caused great sorrow in the Maier home. Yesterday morning she and her two sons attended the services at St. Joseph's church, and afterwards rode in a carriage to the cemetery. After the last rites had been said, Mrs. Maier re-entered her carriage but scarcely had they reached the gates of the cemetery when she groaned and she fell forward. As nothing could be done to revive her they started home, but she died upon reaching the city. Mrs. Maier was born in Germany but came to Milwaukee when but a girl and had always made this her home. She is survived by ten children. Funeral services will be held from the home Sunday afternoon at 2 o'clock. Interment will be at the Union Cemetery.

—*Milwaukee Journal*
October 3, 1902

❖ ❖ ❖

Cold Bath Causes Death
Miss Carrie Davenport Of Beloit Dies Of Heart Failure

BELOIT- Miss Carrie Davenport, aged 45 years, was found dead in a bathtub this morning. She had been in the habit of taking a cold bath each morning and it is thought that the shock of getting the cold water today caused heart failure. For eighteen years, Miss Davenport was a bookkeeper at a local tannery. She was prominent in Methodist church circles.

—*Eau Claire Weekly Telegram*
February 26, 1903

❖ ❖ ❖

Girl Dies For A Poodle
Wisconsin Society Belle Killed By Shock Of Dog's Death

EAU CLAIRE- The death from heart's disease of Miss Nellie Youngs, a pretty society belle, when she saw her favorite poodle ground under the wheels of a fast Northwestern passenger train, may be followed by a formal funeral for the dog as well the girl. Miss Youngs was on Prospect Boulevard as a train passed. The gates across the street were lowered, but

the poodle, which was her companion in the stroll, rushed past them and under the train. Five passenger cars saw the body of her pet on the track. She fainted, dying before a doctor could reach her.

—*Eau Claire Weekly Telegram*
July 30, 1903

❖ ❖ ❖

Yawns Herself To Death
Efforts Of Physicians Fail To Relieve Wisconsin Woman

EAU CLAIRE- After yawning without interruption for three days despite every effort to relieve her, Mrs. William Henry Jenner is dead. Physicians decided that the woman was suffering from obscure lesion of the brain, producing laryngeal spasms. Mrs. Jenner, unable to sleep yawned until she could do so no more from the lack of strength, and then died.

—*Eau Claire Weekly Telegram*
March 26, 1903

❖ ❖ ❖

Father And Son Die Twelve Hours Apart

LAYTON PARK, MILWAUKEE- George Stewart, 71, and Charles Stewart 41, father and son, died twelve hours apart at their home, 1011 Twenty-sixth Avenue, Layton Park. A double funeral will be held from the residence Thursday. The father died of pneumonia, the son of consumption.

—*Milwaukee Journal*
January 18, 1905

❖ ❖ ❖

Man Commits Suicide On Wife's Grave

LA CROSSE- Despondent, presumably because of the loss of his wife and five children during the past three years, Herman Burand, age 53, 1107 S. 3rd Street, committed suicide yesterday afternoon at the graves of his dead family in Oak Grove Cemetery. Burand's body fell over the grave of his wife. Death did not come instantaneously but when help arrived he was breathing his least and appeared to be unconscious of his surroundings.

Yesterday afternoon, shortly after dinner, Mr. Burand left his home and went to the saloon of Gustav Kanard, 1101 S. 3rd Street, where he met a number of friends and told them he was tired of life and would soon be dead. His friends, however, thought nothing of his remarks and afterward Mr. Burand seemed to be more jolly.

Leaving Kanard's saloon, Mr. Burand then went to Henry Einert's grocery store, 1029 S. 4th Street. Here he acted in the same way, telling his friends that they would not see him alive after that evening. He was well acquainted with the butcher in charge of the Einert Meat Market and just before leaving the store he walked into the meat market and told the young man that he had left a cigar for him. Burand then asked Mrs. Einert what strawberries were selling for and upon being told the price he purchased four boxes and left orders to have the berries delivered to his house after 4

o'clock when his children returned home from school.

From Einert's store Burand went to Oak Grove Cemetery, where his wife and five children are buried. A number of visiting delegates from the G.A.R. encampment were then walking through the cemetery seeing the sights. Suddenly they heard the sound of a gunshot. D. Clemens was but a few rods from the scene of the tragedy. He called to R.M. Work, a Civil War veteran from Elroy, who was close by, and together the two men went to where Burand had shot himself. The suicide had fallen over the grave of his wife and close by lay a revolver. The two men raised Burand, who was breathing his last, and a few minutes later he was dead.

—*La Crosse Republican Leader*
June 15, 1905

❖ ❖ ❖

"Dead" Man Really Dies

LA CROSSE- Having lived twenty-five years after being declared dead, John Urbanck, 80, died at Bohemia Ridge, near here. A quarter of a century ago he was struck by a train. The physician believing him dead, performed no other operation than to distend the crushed portions of his skull in preparation for burial.

—*Milwaukee Journal*
January 1, 1906

HIDDEN HEADLINES of WISCONSIN

She Dies
At Sight Of Blood
Baraboo Woman Falls Dead On Scene Of Men's Scuffle

BARABOO- About 11:00 last night during the scuffle, Schuyler Hull was thrown through the plate glass window of Mrs. C.T. Robinson's millinery store and badly cut. Mrs. Robinson was notified of the accident and upon reaching the scene and seeing the blood, dropped dead on the sidewalk was supposed to be due to heart failure.

—Eau Claire Leader
June 12, 1906

❖ ❖ ❖

Dies Of Grief

MARINETTE- Mrs. Le Page, daughter of the late Peter Shepard, who was found dead on the highway under mysterious circumstances, died of grief at Amberg.

—Milwaukee Journal
January 16, 1905

❖ ❖ ❖

Did Grief Kill Her
Succession Of Fatalities In Family Have Caused Death Of Mrs. Laue

MILWAUKEE- Did Mrs. Clara Vogeler Laue, 182 ½ Eleventh Street, die of grief? Her friends believe that she did. The body of her brother, Emil Vogeler, lies in the Gerber undertaking rooms, Chestnut Street, awaiting removal to Chicago for burial, and now the sister is also cold in death.

When her husband, the late Prof. Max Laue, a well known-teacher of vocal music and singer in church choirs of Milwaukee, died a few years ago, leaving her with one child, a boy, her brother came up from Chicago and became her support and protector. When he died a few days ago she was heartbroken and now had joined him in death, leaving her son.

—Milwaukee Journal
January 25, 1908

❖ ❖ ❖

He Sees Death Coming
Man With Strange Presentiment Is Found Dead In Bed

KENOSHA- John Brettner, aged 50, who had a strange premonition of death Thursday when he told the people with whom he was living that he was about to die, was found dead in his bed yesterday morning. He had been a street worker for seven years and left $2,000 in the bank.

—Milwaukee Journal
July 11, 1908

❖ ❖ ❖

Discusses Death;
Drops Dead
Strange Coincidence In Manner Of Death Of Two Little Chute Men

LITTLE CHUTE- Less than five minutes after Martin Weyenberg of Little Chute concluded a conversation about the sudden death of his brother about two years ago, he himself dropped dead at his home yesterday as a result of an attack of heart failure. The conditions surrounding the deaths of the Weyenberg brothers are so similar they are extraordinary. Both men lived to be the same age; both dropped dead from heart failure, neither having had a day's illness for years prior to their death, and both died a short time after discussing the death of another. Martin Weyenberg was one of the most prominent as well as among the wealthiest men in Little Chute, and for a great many years he was chairman of the town.

—Eau Claire Leader Telegram
December 4, 1908

❖ ❖ ❖

Girl Buried Second Time

EAU CLAIRE- The body of Miss Elizabeth School, aged 25, exhumed after having been in the grave for twenty-four hours because neighbors believed that she had been buried before life was extinct, has been reburied.

—Eau Claire Leader
May 26, 1910

HIDDEN HEADLINES of WISCONSIN

HIDDEN HEADLINES of WISCONSIN

Town Haunted House

COOKSVILLE- It is reported that there is a haunted house in town, but his ghost-ship has not shown himself as yet; when he does we will try and be there.

—Janesville Daily Gazette
February 11, 1874

Today the village of Cooksville consists of over 30 historic buildings and sites. The Cooksville Historic District is listed in the National Register of Historic Places and the State Register of Historic Places.

Haunted House

FOOTVILLE- John Wells, having taken unto himself a better half will move into Footville a once. He will occupy the home known as the "haunted house." John is evidently very matter-of-fact, and not the least superstitious.

—Janesville Daily Gazette
January 12, 1881

❖ ❖ ❖

Ghost Story

OSHKOSH- The south side had quite a ghost excitement. The Dowidat or predestination wing of the Evangelical Church that had the split up some ago are erecting a church of their own. Children have been in the habit of playing around the edifice as its construction progressed. One night last week some children were frightened almost out of their wits by seeing a spectral form in white marching through the church. They gave the alarm and others saw it. The figure finally vanished.

The excitement over it spread like wild fire. The superstition brought to mind the church fight of last summer and the fact that several were made crazy by it and began to believe that the appearance of this ghost was in retribution thereof. At any rate such an excitement was awakened that on Friday night upwards of three hundred people gathered about the yard watching for the ghost, but without the satisfaction of seeing it, although every murmur of the wind through the church was constructed as same hollow voice from the grave. The rain of Saturday night prevented any further crowd and the excitement has greatly subsided. It is believed by most people to have been but a practical joke by someone with a white sheet to scare the youngsters who were in the habit of congregating about the building.

—Oshkosh Daily Northwestern
October 9, 1882

❖ ❖ ❖

CHAPTER 2 GHOSTS

Ghost Tale
Is Talk Of Town

LA CROSSE- A ghost story is being so commonly discussed about town that we shall not be accused of peddling horrors if we relate it for the benefit of the few to whom it may yet be news. The ghosts is none of your phosphorescent females wrapped in the cerements of the tomb: it is a male specter with his boots on who takes a lively interest in the railroad business. His haunts are about the Cargill elevator and the general vicinity of the old depot grounds.

His first recorded appearance, date unknown, was to a brakeman standing with a link pin in his hand ready to couple a car to a train backing down towards him. Suddenly the pin disappeared from his hand and was nowhere to be found. The brakeman did not drop it, or throw it; he was in calm possession of all his senses. The pin disappeared as though seized by a strong hand. He saw nobody. We shall not give his name, but if the reader chances to learn it and interrogate him, he will tell about the incident with such calmness and circumstance, with such undoubted conviction of its correctness that no one will feel quite at liberty to say it is all nonsense.

On the ghost's second appearance he was manifest to the eye. He was walking in the track in front of a moving train. The engineer of the train whistled and shouted at the image but "it" paid no heed. Then the engineer strove to stop his train but did not succeed until the engine had overtaken "it." Then the engineer, fireman, and brakeman set out to gather up the remains. To use their own words, they found "neither hide nor hair," though they actually saw the engine strike "it" down and go crushing among "its" diaphanous bones.

Another time a loaded car was uncoupled from a train and sent violently down to the end of the track where it derailed into the sand. No one was near it at the time, and no one human could have started it at all, and no dozen humans could have given it such a velocity. No doubt when anything goes wrong in the yard, "it was the ghost." Several men have been killed by railroad cars in that vicinity and one of them evidently doesn't know that he is discharged and keeps right on about his business the same as ever.

—*La Crosse Chronicle*
November 17, 1882

In 1900, Wisconsin started buying land to create its first state park. That land became Interstate State Park located in St. Croix Falls.

Ghost

EAU CLAIRE- Eau Claire is agitated over the sensation of a haunted house. A vacant store at Mary Dean Slough is the scene of the ghostly apparition.

—*Janesville Gazette*
January 10, 1871

HIDDEN HEADLINES of WISCONSIN

Nocturnal Noises
Explanation Of A Ghost Story That Astonished Some Prominent People Of Eau Claire

EAU CLAIRE- For some nights past those persons who occupy sleeping rooms in business blocks around the corner of Kelsey and Barstow Streets have been considerably surprised by hearing mysterious rappings at regular intervals, between the hours of nine and twelve at night, and stories have been rife about a ghost walking, spiritual manifestations, etc.

As these noises were found to proceed from the boot and shoe store of A.A. Catter, a Leader representative called there yesterday afternoon, and found the proprietor busy at his desk, looking over a large stock of invoices and freight bills. In reply to a query as to what caused the noises in his establishment, Mr. Cutter said that he was receiving a large stock of new goods and that the boys had probably alarmed the neighbors while knocking the covers off boxes and unpacking goods at night after regular business hours.

—*Eau Claire Daily Leader*
August 17, 1883

Kelsey Street no longer exists in Eau Claire as in 1899 a new bridge was built over the river and Kelsey Street was renamed Grand Ave.

A Girl Badly Scared

OSHKOSH- The story is told on the south side that a certain young lady was so badly scared a few nights ago that she has ever since been in a critical condition. The statement is that she is living with a family who occupies a house in which a woman died a short time ago, and being of a nervous and superstitious nature she was constantly in fear of seeing the dead woman's ghost rise up before her.

The other night, as the story goes, she went to a shed or stable in back of the house for some wood, as she opened the door a large dog badly frightened by the unexpected visitor leaped out of the door, knocking her down. She was carried into the house in a hysterical fit and has been in similar condition ever since, with medical aid constantly in attendance. At times, it is stated, when aroused she screams and declares that she still sees the ghost of the dead woman, and it is evident she believed the ghost knocked her down.

—*Oshkosh Daily Northwestern*
October 24, 1883

❖ ❖ ❖

Haunted House

MARINETTE- Marinette has a haunted house which is causing much interest there. Several young men slept in the building recently, but were unable to unravel the mystery.

—*Oshkosh Daily Northwestern*
June 1, 1889

❖ ❖ ❖

Railroad Yard Haunted By Ghost

LA CROSSE- If there is anything in literature that is particularly interesting it is a ghost story. A ghost that is certified by evidence that cannot be disputed is an interesting and fascinating object, and an able-bodied, well-developed ghost, one with aims and objects in life and which has a mission on earth, is sure to hold the attention of even the most skeptical of men.

The *Republican Leader* has such a story to offer to its readers today and it proposes to serve it up on the half shell, with the most absolute assurance that what is hereafter written is the solemn truth. At midnight, when there is an unearthly silence in the River Addition to the City of La Crosse, when naught but the lights of ghastly phosphorescence can be seen moving like ill-omened sparks across the marsh, and when every glimmer that pierces the awful gloom of night seems to come stealing through the air from some lonely gravestone, at this unseemly hour when every honest ghost should be asleep, there appears a ghastly phantom on the railroad track near the elevators.

The specter paces back and forth along the iron rails in shadowy garments that fade away and then reappear as if the night winds held them in their keeping. For many nights this strange creation from the other world has haunted this fateful spot. His shadowy form has hovered silently and mysteriously among the gloomy box-cars that stand in the track, or it has stood like a dim specter upon the tender of a switch engine and showed its corpse-like

features to the terrified trainmen on the engine. At these fearful moments, the trainmen have brushed the cinders from their eyes and gazed at each other, wondering, no doubt, if this was but the wild hallucination of an ardent spirit, or if the restless soul of some unfortunate railroad man had been doomed to walk the earth and make night work a burden to the men still on the payroll of the La Crosse division. It is undoubtedly the latter.

The ghost first appeared here two years ago and was seen by hundreds. It seemed to predict an accident at every appearance. Man after man quit the service of the yard foreman. They could not pass that awful spot, seeing the grinning skull of a disembodied spirit, feel the indescribable touch of an unseen hand, and worst of all come to know that the cursed ghost was following the shivering brakeman the length of the train, pulling coupling pins as fast as they were put in.

At last the ghost disappeared, and a few brave men were found who stayed on the payroll and worked the area. But alas for human hopes, the ghost has now reappeared and the trouble has commenced. It is known that no less than 10 railroad men have been killed near this spot since the track was laid. As many more have drowned while within a few feet of the ghost's haunt, and it was near here where the steamer War Eagle burned in 1870, claiming several lives. The associations of the place are uncanny.

Last night as a brakeman was about to couple a carload of wheat into a train, and before he had given the signal to "back up 10 feet," he was dumbfounded to see the box car gradually approaching him, moved by unseen hands. He wondered and shook with fear, but made the coupling. The train was ready to pull out, the signal was given and the engine started. Not a car moved. Every pin had been silently pulled from the links more swiftly than four brakemen could accomplish. It was the ghost. There is no longer any doubt in it. What his object can be is a mystery. It is evident he wants something to appease his soul's desire.

The *Republican Leader* hopes for the best but awaits future events with untold anxiety. In the meantime it advises all the railroad men to stand by their couplings and not let their hair stand on end even if they are able swing their lanterns clear through a dozen apparitions who may hover around that ghostly region. It may be a spirit that wants a job.

—*La Crosse Republican*
October 28, 1884

Ghost Removed Bedding And Unlocked Doors

LA CROSSE- A new sensation in the line of ghosts has appeared on the north side. Arthur Anderson, an engineer in the Goddard mill, has been living in the house known as the "Sly property" on Liberty Street, and claims that the house is haunted, and, moved out today as a consequence.

The apparition made itself known by removing bedding, unbolting doors, dis-

turbing books, and performing other such capers. It is claimed these things do happen and at times when lights have been left burning, and that Mr. Anderson's family is not the first in the house to have been disturbed by the ghost. Mrs. Anderson, who is not very strong in constitution, is nearly sick because of the fright she had received.

The house was watched last night and will be watched again tonight. This is the main topic of conversation today instead of the roller skating rinks.

—*La Crosse Republican*
March 20, 1885

❖ ❖ ❖

Haunted House

MONROE- It is reported that there is a haunted house in the south part of town that is haunted. For the past few years several families have lived there for only a short time each, and report the house being visited by a genuine ghost. The being, or whatever it is, only visits the house at nights, and the people who lived there are unable to describe it, only that there are strange rappings at the doors and all night's tramping all over the house. We should judge from the looks of the doors and windows, that the devil held forth there instead of a ghost. It is further reported that the cellar has been used as a grave yard. If this is the case no wonder they see strange objects and hear awful noises at night.

—*The Monroe Independent*
November 24, 1890

Ghosts
In the Next County

NORWAY- The superstitious are excited over a ghost story coming from the town of Norway, or rather what may be more properly termed, a strange phenomena, in the appearance of human faces in a window pane. The strange sight is said to be witnessed at the farm house occupied by Thos. Mealy, which for years was the home of a rich and eccentric couple known as William and Torena Gregg, but now deceased.

The lineaments of human faces are depicted or caricatured on the window panes, one of which so closely resembles that of a deceased Mr. Gregg that his old neighbors recognize it as his likeness. It is claimed that this likeness appeared about six months ago, but the other one has been noticed for several years. This is the story as told, and many curious people have visited the place.

—Waukesha Freeman
August 31, 1893

Ghost Appears As
Woman In White

LA CROSSE- A well authenticated ghost story is being told in the First Ward and the entire neighborhood there is greatly excited. The ghost was seen by two ladies who tell the same story the occurrence, and to many it seems very mysterious.

The ghost or spirit was seen last Friday night and the circumstances were as follows: The lady of the house is the wife of a traveling salesman and is left alone much of the time. For some time past she has been residing in rented housing and finally decided to move, which she did last Friday. Her husband being away she had a woman friend come to the house for the night.

During the night the lady of the house was awakened by something unknown, and was astonished to see a woman in white standing by the bedside, while in one of the corners of the room a bright light was seen close to the ceiling. The lady woke her companion and the two saw the white figure cross the room three times and then disappear. The mysterious light went out at the same time and the ladies were left in a state of mind which is easier imagined than described. The neighbors are awaiting further developments.

—La Crosse Republican
August 24, 1891

❖ ❖ ❖

Palmyra's
Haunted House

PALMYRA- Palmyra has a haunted house located on the Cushman farm, on the outskirts of the village. One of the forms which the apparition takes is that of a woman in black who raps at the front door and when it is opened vanishes into thin air. The present tenants, John Higgins and wife, have become weary of the demonstrations and are about to move out.

—Waukesha Freeman
December 17, 1896

CHAPTER 2 GHOSTS

"Haunted House" Burned

Resort Where Ross Murdered His Wife And Her Sister

KAUKAUNA- What was known as the "haunted house" since the Ross murder was committed in it was burned last night near this city. The place was situated nearly east of Kaukauna on the Wrightstown road. It was wooden and was owned by Mrs. Beaulien, who had a tenant in it. The insurance on the building is $400 and on the furniture, also owned by Mrs. Beaulien $200. This is the famous place where Ross shot his wife, her sister, a male companion who accompanied them.

—*Sheboygan Times*
August 28, 1897

❖ ❖ ❖

Oshkosh Has A Haunted House
The Ghost Of Murdered Birdie Fox Said To Frequent Her Former Home

Queer Stories Told By The Neighbors Of Strange Sights Seen At Night

George Mills Under Bonds On Charge Of Killing His Sweetheart

OSHKOSH- Not everyone in Oshkosh is a skeptic in the manifestation of spirits, for not a few people are certain that Birdie Fox, who, it is alleged was slain by the hand of her lover last July, reappears night after night at 371 Jefferson Street, the house in which she met her untimely end.

Birdie was not what the world calls a good girl—she was something on the order of Nancy, immortalized by Dickens in his *Oliver Twist*. She loved George Mills with a misguided passion and paid for her devotion with her life. Since her murder last July, the home in which she met her untimely end has been the scene of queer happenings and uncanny festivities.

On certain nights, the neighbors say the rooms blaze with a myriad of lights from cellar to garret and they are suddenly extinguished. Again, one room will instantly be lighted up and remain illumined for the whole night. White, flitting shadows have been seen to dance before the windows and seem to beckon to the frightened neighbors to come in and call on the neighbors from the spirit land. No noises ever accompany the ghostly revels and in many ways the spooks are models. They have never borrowed a harp nor a lawn mower from any of their neighbors, although they appear very capricious, seeming to have just as good of a time in the cellar as they do in the garret.

A family moved into the house last summer, but remained only about month. They did not seem to be able to get on the right side of Birdie's ghost and suddenly moved out. Some skeptics have gone so far as to say that "It is cheaper to see ghosts than to pay the rent."

The ghost may be avenged shortly as the case of George Mills, her alleged murderer, will be tried next Tuesday in the circuit court. On the night of July 13 last shots were heard by the inmates of the house in the room occupied by Birdie Fox. The girls rushed immediately to her and found her dying on the bed. On the floor near her lay George Mills, with two bullet wounds in the breast, gasping for breath. The girl lived until 8 o'clock the next morning, but did not recover consciousness long enough to make an ante mortem statement. Mills was taken to the hospital in what was supposed to be a dying condition but his wonderful vitality rendered his attempt on his own life unsuccessful. He was finally nursed back to health and then arrested, charged with the murder of the girl. He is at present out on bail in the sum of $6,000. It is understood that an affidavit of prejudice of presiding judge will be filed and that an effort will be made to have the case go over to the next term.

—Milwaukee Journal
January 6, 1899

❖ ❖ ❖

Ghosts In Fremont

FREMONT- The old Clow house in Fremont is said to be haunted. Among the stories told is this one: Occupants hear strange sounds, beginning in the upper room with noises such as a scuffle, then a fall, then seemingly a heavy body is dragged over the kitchen floor down the stairs and ended at last by a sound as though a body had been thrown into the well which is under the kitchen. The family is frightened as are others who have stayed and kept vigil through the night. One evening when the struggle in one of the upper rooms had begun the watchers waited awhile, then taking a lamp rushed in. Something seemed to fall but they

found an empty room. No one can account for the supernatural sounds and movements within the dwelling. Neighbors tell the same story as do the family. They will move out at once for more congenial company than ghosts.

—Marion Advertiser
February 2, 1900

Palmyra Ghost Resumes Business

The Cushman House Again The Scene Of Its Appearance.
Country Folk All Believe It Is A Supernatural Visitor.
Story Of A Threat To Haunt The Premises Made By Order.

PALMYRA- After an absence of several months the ghost of Mrs. J. R. Cushman, which for four years has haunted the Cushman house in the outskirts of Palmyra, had again made its appearance, and it was seen recently by George Greenwood, a thoroughly reliable and temperate citizen whom the ghost followed a mile along the road skirting the spook house.

Although the styles have changed much since the ghost went into business, it still wears the same brown coat that it did four years ago, and inasmuch as it is a woman ghost, this utter contempt of things material and modern is the strongest evidence that it is indeed ethereal. No one with any self-respect, leastwise a woman, would ever impersonate a ghost which wore such a fright of a coat. Therefore it must be a real ghost.

However, it differs from other self-respecting ghosts only in the color of its coat. It works on the liquid air principle, dissolving into thin air after the regular number of ghostly calisthenics. It pounds on the door, writes messages in Mrs. Cushman's handwriting, and walks around on all the loose boards in the house. In this it displays absolutely no originality, but has the matter of noises down to such a fine point that a half dozen families have moved in the house only to move out again after the ghost signified its disapproval.

The Cushmans lived on the farm twenty-five years, during which time it is said there was considerable wrangling about whom should eventually come into possession of it. Four years ago Mrs. Cushman died. She wanted the farm to go to her favorite son, Charles, and declared that if it did not go to him she would haunt the house ever after. Fred got the farm. He rented part of it and immediately afterward queer things began to happen. One night a piece of paper, evidently torn from the wall, floated in with this message written in the hand of Mrs. Cushman upon it: "He tried to kill me today."

All the good work of the ghost at this time was credited to Charles who was still in the vicinity, but since then he has moved away and the mysterious happenings still continue. Each family has moved away and the mysteriously happenings still continue. Each family that has moved in since of the Woman in Brown, whereupon they immediately moved out.

Mr. Higgins, one of the tenants, was found dead in his barn shortly after he moved in. Heart disease was said to be the cause, but those who believed in ghosts thought differently. Strange as it may seem a large majority of the people here believe the implicitly in the existence of the ghost, and the house has been visited by people for miles around. Now that it has come back ghost parties will be a feature of local interest for the next few weeks.

—*Milwaukee Journal*
February 19, 1900

❖ ❖ ❖

Saw A Specter

MILWAUKEE- Colored residents of the Fourth Ward near 316 Well Street claim they have seen the ghost of Cora Jones, suicide, and some in the vicinity are said to be moving away.

—*Milwaukee Journal*
October 5, 1900

❖ ❖ ❖

Weird Tale Told About Haunted Cabin

BAD AXE- Haunted houses in fiction are common, but here is one that is really the abiding place of spooks, and river men on the upper Mississippi and residents in the vicinity of Devil's Elbow, near which it is located, avoid it as they would the plague. Years ago James Hubbel erected a log house close to the river. His wife was an Indian woman and to them were born two children.

For years the Indian woman proved a faithful wife. Then her love fled with the coming of one of her old-time red skinned admirers, and between them a conspiracy was planned to murder Hubbel and the two children. One night Hubbel was seized by his wife and her Indian lover, bound and tied to a tree while the children were drowned before his eyes. As they sank beneath the water the agonized father swore that living or dead he would make life hell upon earth for the murderers.

He was struck over the head by the man who had robbed him of his wife and children, and as he fell forward a knife was plunged into his breast by the woman. About a year after the murder river men who stopped at the cabin while running logs down the river found the woman dead in her bed, while the body of the Indian was found on the floor, with a bullet hole in the head. How they came to their death was never determined.

Ever since that time strange sounds, as of children wailing, and a man moaning in mortal agony, have been heard about the place, and the river men say they have seen white forms coming and going around the place. Last fall two hunters made camp at the cabin and tried to sleep there. During the night they were awakened by strange sounds and driven from the place in terror, by the appearance of what they say were the ghosts of children.

That there is something uncanny about the place is shown by the fact that even timber wolves do not prowl about the hut, and bears give it a wide berth. Attempts have been made to burn the cabin, but each time the fire has been extinguished in a mysterious manner.

—*Milwaukee Journal*
January 26, 1901

The area around Bad Axe was the location for the Battle (Massacre) of Bad Axe. In 1832, members of the Sauk Tribe were surrendering to U.S. Troops when apparently, due to miscommunication, Lt. Kingsley ordered the troops to open fire on the tribe. When the smoke cleared, over 20 Sauk had been killed.

Ghost Haunts Bedside of Murdered Girl

WAUSAU- Another chapter has developed in the case of Jacob Schaumburger, the young man who last fall accidentally killed his sweetheart and subsequently was sentenced to five years in state's prison. The heart rendering details of that tragedy are being refreshed in the minds of relatives of the principals by alleged nightly visits of a ghost of the murdered girl, which comes from a cellar, carries a small night lamp and seats itself on the side of the victim's bed. In hopes of escaping these dreadful visits the family has vacated the house. There is considerable uneasiness in that section of the city over the revelation which is credited by many.

—*Milwaukee Journal*
April 1, 1902

❖ ❖ ❖

Spook, Crank, or Masker
Apparition On North Side Hill Causes Great Stir Last Night. Ghostly Object Seemed To Some Like Man Dressed As A Woman.

EAU CLAIRE- Reports came to Sergt. Elliot of the Eau Claire police force at a late hour last night that attention of the police was required in the residence district of the North-side hill, where it was a number of women had been scared by a person in the garb of a woman who was parading around residence streets and acting in a particular manner. The party was described as of large build and carrying a fan. The supposition of some was that "it"

was a man or boy dressed as a woman, and either crazy or bent on mischievous pranks. When Sergt. Elliot arrived in the locality where the supposed masquerader had been seen "it" had disappeared from the scene. Another account shows that the mysterious masquerader if he or she was such, was seen by the Sisters of the Scared Heart school dodging around the church and school house between 9 and 10 o'clock last night; that the Sisters were very much alarmed; that a lot of people gathered near the school to watch the gyrations of the mysterious "critter" who, when an attempt was made to approach him, her, or it, the capture was impossible. Some of the youngsters who believe in spooks think that "it" is the real thing in the line of ghosts.

—*Eau Claire Weekly Telegram*
July 31, 1902

❖ ❖ ❖

Auburn Village Has A Mystery
Unexplained Moans And Cries At A Lake House Cause Much Excitement. Sounds Apparently Come From Marsh Near Omaha Road. Investigation.

AUBURN VILLAGE- The world is full of mysteries. Some are solved, some remain clouded for all time. The people of Auburn had one last evening that continues to keep some of them guessing. Considerable excitement and wide speculation was occasioned in the little village at a late hour last night, and since that time it

has been the chief topic of conversation on the streets there. About 10 o'clock, or shortly after the arrival of a late freight from the south, the excitement occurred. Loud shrieks and screams, seemingly those of a woman or child in great stress or despair, startled all pedestrians and loungers about who were out at that hour.

The sounds came from the southwest of the village. This is a low marshy section and just such a place would arouse the suspicions of the people there that some appalling tragedy has occurred. The land is covered with the thick underbrush and is in close proximity to the Omaha railroad track. The first supposition was that someone had either fallen off a bridge or been struck by the freight train, which had passed just before the queer sound had been heard.

The suspicions of Mr. Sayer of that village became aroused to that extent that he in company with a number of friends, went down along the right of way for a distance of half a mile or more for the purpose of making an investment. Lanterns were taken, but the curious party was unable to solve the problem or get any response to their yells. The party returned to the village. Soon after they were given surprise No. 2 by hearing the same hideous cries and moans which were louder than the first, coming from the woods, apparently about half a mile from the railroad truck. Several of the prominent citizens of Auburn procured lanterns and marched forth to take up the search anew, which was not concluded till some time after the midnight hour, and then it was abandoned only on account of the rain.

While the search was fruitless, many believe the cried were those of some person who had been badly injured or was demented. Others less sensationally inclined are of the belief that it was some animal, only that and nothing more. The Heralds informant, who is one of the leading business men of Auburn feels quite confident that developments will follow that will disprove the latter theory.

—*Eau Claire Weekly Leader*
August 7, 1902

❖ ❖ ❖

Says Spooks Are Seen Where Body Was Found

FOND DU LAC– Since the discovery of the box of human bones in the old Post building, the structure has been one of the especial interest to many. Several who have kept vigil over the property at night report that they have seen strange lights and shadowy forms moving about the building.

—*Milwaukee Journal*
October 8, 1902

❖ ❖ ❖

Racine Ghost

RACINE- People in the north side of the river at Racine are excited over the discovery of a haunted house, located on Superior Street and owned by John Relman. It was the home of a midwife, but some months ago she died. The widower remained and a family moved in. The family suddenly moved out of the place, giving no explanation. Then two families from Ohio moved in. They are convinced that the place is haunted.

—*Wisconsin State Journal*
November 13, 1902

❖ ❖ ❖

The Racine Ghost
Not A Woman in White This Time, But A Woman In Black.
People Swoon When They See Her.

RACINE- *The Racine Journal* has made an investigation. While it is impossible with a few minutes time to have all the stories substantiated, they were well founded. It is now claimed that a young lady, residing on Douglas Avenue, who was chased by this hideous individual, is now suffering with nervous prostration. The attending physician states his patient is in a critical state. It is impossible to make a canvass of the residents of that section and ascertain just where the young lady lived, but the story came from such a responsible source that it is given a good deal of credence.

It seems that the young lady was walking home, without an escort a few evenings ago when she was accosted by this fearful being, who wore a black shroud with a heavy black veil. The many weird gestures, frightened the young lady into a state of mental collapse. She managed to break away from the character and run frantically to her home, where she fell into a swoon. She revived sufficiently, however, to tell her experience. Other parties claim to have seen the person although "it" seldom attacks anybody but woman. A prominent west sider who saw the stranger, gave chase, but was not fleet of foot enough to overtake the character.

The "woman in black" broke and ran and when "she" raised her skirts at a street crossing a man's trousers suggested that the individual is a man in disguise. It is generally believed that the "woman in black" is a degenerate. It does not seem possible that a person with a sound mind could resort to such escapades. The people in that section are going after this fellow and, fool or no fool, unless the practice is stopped immediately he will be wounded and subjected to a nice coat of tar and feathers and then given a ride on a rail.

—*Eau Claire Leader*
March 22, 1904

❖❖❖

Ghost Haunted
Suicide Site

LA CROSSE- For some time the residents near the corner of Wood and Loomis Streets have been alarmed nightly by the mysterious appearances and disappearances of an object apparently of phantom form which exists in the Holmbo residence, 1419 Logan Street.

It is reported that the Holmbo house is brilliantly lighted every night and that an object shrouded in white appears at the windows swinging its arms and going through various gesticulations. The situation has caused no little uneasiness among the residents of that vicinity, as several

searchers have been made of the property with nothing being found.

Last year (August 1, 1904) Nicolai Holmbo committed suicide by hanging himself on that property and since that time the house has been vacant. The wild cries and frantic gestures of the object attract the attention of passersby every night, but the exceedingly bright lights in the house are extinguished as soon as anyone enters the yard. A number of men residing in the neighborhood have visited the house several times at night when the phantom was at a window, but each time as they reach the gate the lights go out and the cries cease.

Through a through search has been made of the house each night, nothing can be found and a deathly quiet prevails. An investigation is pending.

—*La Crosse Chronicle*
May 27, 1905

❖❖❖

Did Spooks Do It
Or Was it
Spontaneous Combustion.
A Remarkable Case On Broadway.

EAU CLAIRE- Mr. O. J. Arnstad, the carpenter, a brother of Ole Arnstad, the contractor, is up against it, or rather was up against it Saturday night. How could his cellar stairs and cellar way take fire without his knowing it? O.J. wishing to bring a bottle of his celebrated Juniper beer from the cellar, lamp in hand descended. On his way down he noticed in the wall a rubber

brush, a small mirror and a few other articles of toilet.

Everything was calm and still and quiet. Having secured his bottle he ascended, but no sooner than he arrived in the kitchen than his little son Johnnie, aged 11, exclaimed; "Oh, Pa, I smell smoke!" The whole family rushed to the cellar door and to their horror found everything in flames.

The rubber brush, towel, and other articles were blazing on the floor. Mr. Arnstad luckily had his shoes on, so he jumped on them putting them out. Mrs. Arnstad and Jonnie ran with pails of water and soon it was discovered there was no need to run to the box at the corner of Sixth Avenue and Broadway.

Some of the neighbors feel satisfied there is and had been for many years a ghost on that cellar. It must be either that or else a clear case of spontaneous combustion brought about by the rubber brush colliding with the towel and both getting mixed up with celluloid back comb which was also close by.

—*Eau Claire Leader*
December 20, 1905

Police Seek For Ghosts
Kenosha Officers Watch In Vain For Figure Which Scared Women

KENOSHA- The Kenosha police were called out at midnight this morning to hunt a ghost which was alleged to be moving about the Kenosha city cemetery. The army of bluecoats advanced against the supposed spirit, but it failed to put in an appearance. Several people testified to seeing the spirit in the cemetery at midnight.

It was alleged that it was a flesh and blood "ghost" and that it had taken this practical joke on some women friends. Several of the women who saw the alleged spirit are suffering from hysteria.

—*Eau Claire Leader*
August 18, 1905

❖ ❖ ❖

Weird Tale Of Haunted House
Former Owner Drives In And Goes Through Act Of Unhitching. Phantoms Thrill Third Ward House Holder. Great Interest In Mystery.

EAU CLAIRE- The Third Ward has a haunted house story! A weird tale this, that sends thrills chasing up and down the spinal column, and causes each separate hair to stand on end like the quills of that much quoted and virulent porcupine. According to neighborhood gossip the haunted house is that very handsome residence erected not long ago by Mrs. Oramel Walker, at the corner of Barstow and Emery Streets, and now inhabited by Ex–Alderman Louis Schmidt, a gentleman known far and wide for his gentle disposition and kindly nature.

No better or more thought of citizen ever trod the streets of Eau Claire than the late

Oramel Walker. In the early days, when Barstow Street was still a shambling lane, Oramel Walker erected a pleasant home for those days—a palatial home—and commodious barns for his stock. That region, now known as the aristocratic Third, was fine farming country in those days. Mr. Walker saw a prosperous city grow up about him. His rolling acres were cut up into town lots and lanes were succeeded by well laid out streets and avenues. Homes sprung up like magic. His pleasant farmhouse became a city dwelling and his splendid barns found themselves on the corner of Barstow and Emery Streets and amenable to road and property tax in the noble Third Ward.

Years rolled on, as years have a habit of doing. Oramel Walker, and his house, and his barns, grew old together. They became landmarks in the midst of a thriving, progressive, and aggressive city. Fine homes were built and old ones were rebuilt around him. As the story goes, Mrs. Walker importuned, for architects and contractors, but Mr. Walker, old associates being dearer to him than grandeur, did not want his home or his barns changed from their original design.

The grim reaper came, and Mr. Walker was no more.

After the lapse of time the widow carried out her long cherished plans of remodeling. She sold the old homestead to the Methodists. They rebuilt the house, making it into a model parsonage. The barns adjoining them were then demolished, and a handsome home arose in their place, most of the well-seasoned and perfectly sound timber being used in the reconstruction.

For a time Mrs. Walker lived there herself. According to the story, she became desirous of selling. Louis Schmidt became the purchaser. Stories of ghosts spread through the neighborhood. Uncanny tales are told. Tales of strange rappings and unaccountable noises. One story is that the shade of the late Mr. Walker drives his famous coal black team—now phantom horses—through the side of the house, and unharnesses them in the dining room. There is stamping of horses' feet and commands of "Whoa!" "Get over there!" are heard, much to the distress of the material occupants. Some of the neighbors don't believe in ghosts; some of them do. All of them are awed and the *Leader* tells the story as it has been told to it by several.

—*Eau Claire Leader*
January 7, 1906

❖ ❖ ❖

Haunted House Is Sold Under Hammer
Beloit's Mysterious Building Purchased By John P. Neill Of Waunakee Today For $3,900

BELOIT- To satisfy a mortgage held by the Merchants & Mechanics' bank of Janesville the old Preston house property located on Sixth Street in Beloit, was this morning purchased at sheriff's sale by John P. Neill of Waunakee, Dane County, Wisconsin. The consideration was $3,900.

The house was built before the Civil War

by Dr. Sanderson, a southerner, who tradition says, was a counterfeiter. It contains twenty-four rooms, a basement and wine cellar. It is also said to have been equipped with trap doors, secret passages, etc., which lends color to the counterfeit tradition. Dr. Sanderson left there at the opening of the war and soon after word came that he was shot and killed in St. Louis. He had a family but all trace of it has been lost. The house had the reputation of being haunted, but during the occupancy of the late O.B. Carpenter, F.L. Preston and others, no one seems to have seen the ghost walk. Mr. and Mrs. E.C. Everett are the present occupants.

—*Janesville Daily Gazette*
January 18, 1906

❖ ❖ ❖

Ask Police To Rid House Of Ghosts

EAU CLAIRE- Mr. and Mrs. Charles Berg believe that their home is haunted and have asked the police to catch the ghosts. They claim that furniture is moved from one part of their home to the other, where they are temporarily, and no one is ever seen about the house. Watches and jewelry, also money is never touched.

—*Eau Claire Leader*
March 1, 1906

❖ ❖ ❖

And Now Comes A Ghost Story
From Nashotah, An Unexplainable Phenomena. Testimony Said To Be Unimpeachable.

NASHOTAH- The following are extracts from Nashotah to the Minneapolis Journal: Rev. William Lloyd Breck was known as "The Pioneer of the Church," in Episcopalian circles. After he founded the Seabury mission, he went on to California, where he established St. Augustine's college for boys, and St. Mary's of the Pacific for girls, at Benicia. He died and was buried there. Several years later, the Wisconsin church asked that his body be transferred to the scene of his early labors and it was exhumed and brought to Nashotah.

After his arrival the casket containing the remains lay for a time on the ground floor of one of the seminary buildings, where each night watchers sat with it until the time for the ceremonies attending the reburial should arrive. On the night before these ceremonies, the watchers were Rev. James Ashmun of Chicago, and Rev. Charles P. Dorset, at the time of his death presiding over a parish in Texas, but then and until within the last few years as a resident of La Crosse, Wis. Along in the hours toward morning, the Chicago clergymen left the building for a little turn in the fresh air, but in a moment came rushing back with the exclamation: "Dorset, Dorset, and the woods are full of ghosts." Both clergymen went out. In every direction through the trees they saw figures flitting hither and thither in a wild and fitful dance. The clergymen approached them, but the figures in front drew back, moving off to the left and right of them. The clergymen asked themselves several questions. Had the farming population of the lonely neighborhood turned out to dance there in the small hours of the morning in the seminary woods? Were the Staid theological students out at an unseemly hour, on a night made solemn as the eve of the reburial of the founder of the school? And even if farmers or students had been moved to do such strange things, where did they get the untiring strength that made these creatures in the woods dance so constantly and so lightly?

The clergymen did not believe the apparitions were men, nor did they afterwards learn that anybody had been abroad in the woods at that time. They were convinced that the figures were ghosts, or that some strange phantasmagoria had deceived not one mind, but two, which an illusion does not often do. But the strange experience of the watchers had not ended. In the morning when the casket was moved, there was a round hole burned through the floor on the spot where the casket stood. A heap of old papers underneath the floor also had been burned. Had fire found its way underneath the building to this spot in the mass of paper, and so up through the floor? Perhaps. The freaks of the real are often as strange as anything we attribute to the unreal.

But several things must be noted. If the fire came in under the floor from without, it escaped setting fire to other debris in its progress. Moreover, the appearance of the hole and the area of burned paper seemed to indicate that the fire had burned from above downward, like the ray of a burning glass. How did the fire come to burn the hole under the casket, which, it must be explained, rested directly upon the floor? A few nights later, the faculty of the institution sat in the office of Dr. Gardner, the president, discussing the recent mystifying events. Suddenly their discussion was terminated by a tremendous racket just outside the door. Waiting a moment in the hope it would cease, Dr. Gardner threw open the door. The noise ceased instantly. All was silent and dark in the hall. Whoever it was had taken himself off with a rapidity that was astounding. Three times more the noise was resumed and three times it ceased as the door was jerked open and two searchers of the building failed to discover in it a living soul except the members of the facility. When Dr. Gardner had looked out a fourth time upon an untenanted corridor, he said, "If you are gentlemen, you will cease this disturbance." It did not begin again.

In any other than a theological school, such a manifestation would be assigned to a very natural cause, but there is the presumption that theological students do not indulge in such inseemly pranks. While students might play tricks upon their own number in their own lodging, it seemed strange that they should go into another building to annoy their faculty. Between believing in ghosts and the impeccability of clerical neophytes, it must be said many of the clergy incline to attribute the disturbance to ghosts, while the students themselves in relating this tale, say it is a queer magnifying of a trivial student joke, unseemly, to be sure, but one which some postulant for holy orders did not perpetrate.

After the burial of Dr. Beck, a photograph was taken of the cemetery of the seminary. One of the students was the photographer. In the foreground of the picture can be seen two graves, just as they appear in the cemetery. But at the foot of each grave stands its occupant, Rev. Dr. Cole former president of the seminary, in full canonical. At the foot of the other, stands the counterfeit presentment of its occupant, a lady who during life was a benefactor of the seminary. As in many other unexplainable phenomena, we may dismiss all these queer tales of a theological seminary by repudiating the testimony purporting to substantiate them. At Nashotah no one does this. At Nashotah, the testimony is believed to be unimpeachable.

—*Eau Claire Leader*
July 3, 1906

❖ ❖ ❖

North Side Ghosts Seen
A Young Lady Preyed Upon By A Devouring Curiosity.
Visits Haunted House.
Hears Chains Rattle.
See Spirits Of Indian Chief.

"Angels and ministers of grace defend us! Be thou a spirit of health, or goblin damned. Bring with thee airs from heaven or blasts from hell, Be thy intents wicked or charitable, Thou comest in such a questionable shape." – Hamlet.

EAU CLAIRE- A young lady well known in society, accompanied by two friends, preyed upon by a devouring curiosity visited the haunted house last night and on her return called the *Leader* office and related her experience. She said: "I was determined to investigate this ghost matter that has appeared in the paper having always taken a great interest in such matters.

Although I cannot say that I believe in either spirits or spiritualism. Still my faith has been staggered not only by what I have read but by what I have seen. I therefore embraced the opportunity of the paper mill ghost, if I may so call it to give the matter an overt test. I easily persuaded two of my companions to go with me. I do not want their names mentioned and you must not mention mine to any one as I would be pestered to death both personally and by phone. Well, we went to the house. My companions hung back. I walked boldly up to the front door and put my first my ear and then my eye to the keyhole. I heard or thought I heard chains rattle, and I saw or imagined I saw an Indian chief or what looked like an Indian chief in the passage. This was quite enough for me for one night. I beat a speedy retreat and together with my companions we put as much space as possible between us and that house. I certainly would not care to repeat the visit. This is all I know. You can make what you like out of it, but remember, no names."

Note by Reporter: This undoubtedly is the spirit of "Big Heart," the famous chief who, in conjunction with Mrs. Handley plundered people here out of $7,000, through the medium of Salted Silver Mine at Porterville, four miles from Eau Claire. The matter is still fresh in the minds of hundreds, yes, thousands here, and some of the victims are still alive. It was one of the most transparent swindles ever perpetrated in Wisconsin and beat Cassie Chadwick all to pieces. Can it be possible that the old chief is trying to get into the corporosity of some speculative lady in this city? Let the down trodden tax payers be on the look out.

—*Eau Claire Leader*
July 21, 1906

❖ ❖ ❖

Ghosts
Much In Evidence
House On North Side Said To Be Frequented
By Beings Of Other World.
Furniture Moves; Chairs Rock;
And Footsteps Are
Plainly Heard By Residents.

EAU CLAIRE- Mothers who use the old story of the "bogy" man to frighten their children with can find the genuine article in a house on the North side if reports can be believed, for it is said that a certain house opposite the paper mill is nightly visited by ghostly beings of the other world who indulge in all sort of pranks, not excepting the groans, etc…, that are always part and parcel of a first-class ghost story. For some time people have moved into this house and as quickly or more so, moved out again, and around the city that the house is haunted.

To those that indulge themselves in the belief that the residents of the other world return to this sphere and visit the scenes of their credence, but to the popular mind some other cause is assigned for the noises and other things that take place there. A short time ago a lady with a good-sized family moved here from Duluth and rented the house in question, and after living there just about long enough to get the furniture in place moved again, ascribing as a reason that it was too far from her son's work, but to those on the inside it was whispered that there had been visitations and noises that she was unable to account for, and of so unearthly a nature that she had decided to move. Other families have from time to time moved into the house, and as quickly moved out again. Asked as to their reasons for so summarily moving, they have all told the same story of moving furniture, chairs rocking when no one was near them, and of footsteps, groans, etc. being heard.

The matter of the haunted house has caused much comment and lately several of the more venturesome of the young men of the city have gone to the house with the avowed intention of staying all night. A few nights ago a member of the police department in response to several requests went to the house and remained until midnight, but neither saw or heard anything, but it is said that on Wednesday evening a couple of young men went there and as one of them was ascending the stairs to the upper floor, her received a resounding slap on the face that put him out for about fifteen minutes.

This much is sure—haunted or not haunted—all who have attempted to live in the house have heard and seen the same phenomena, and be the ghosts real or bogus they have got them all scared. It is extremely likely that someone is making his home there and does not care to be compelled to move to other quarters where perhaps the landlord may not be afraid of ghosts and will appear and demand the rent.

—*Eau Claire Leader*
July 20, 1906

Think The Ghost Of Woman Haunts Bridge

CHRISTIE- That a certain bridge crossing the Black River in the town of Christie is haunted is the scene of the accident. As many as eight vicinity. Some believe that it is the ghost of Mrs. John Mills, who was drowned at that point last fall, who is visiting the scene of the accident. As many as eight farmers have seen what they believe to be the ghost. The subject is being discussed in almost every household in that neighborhood, and while there are a number of skeptics, there are many who take stock in the visions that have come to farmers.

—*Eau Claire Leader*
December 27, 1907

❖ ❖ ❖

Was It A Spook?

EAU CLAIRE- At Park Place Thursday night, as Ralph Atkinson and younger Fletcher, son of Dr. Fletcher, were discussing a new kind of rubber band, that sends peas and pellets with an unerring certainty into the corners of eyes, ears, and etc., their ears were assailed with a terrible clash, and most unheard of noise. Ralph dashed back into the house, and Fletcher fled in all directions. Having fastened the doors the young major ran for the Leader office with "Oh pa!" this and "Oh pa!" that. "Well my boy," was the reply, "If it is as bad as that, we'll just take Officer Johnson with us, and we three will be in Park Place in a jiffy, and the ghost or whatever it is had better shuffle off again."

HIDDEN HEADLINES of WISCONSIN

Owing to over-crowded Interurbans that memorable fair day and night, the Third Ward cars were putting in "dead-licks" to make up time, but they couldn't go too fast for our purpose. On the way up Policeman Johnson remarked: "I never had no faith in ghosts." Conductor Roy Vaughn differed with him materially, and was on speaking terms with a respectable elderly ghost and a couple of goblins near the corner of Bellinger and Randall. After putting his car in the barn and on his way to his home, especially during the dark of the moon, it was Roy's custom to whistle most of the way in order to keep his courage up. Arriving at Park Place, as soon as the stable lantern was obtainable the following was the order of procession.

—*Eau Claire Leader*
September 26, 1906

❖ ❖ ❖

A Bloody Locality
Near Appleton Is Place The Scene Of Many Tragic Happenings

APPLETON- The neighborhood about the Michael McCarty farm has the unenviable record of the most violent deaths of any tract of land of its dimensions in Wisconsin, for it has to its discredit six murders, five deaths on a railroad crossing, and one other accidental death, not to mention the latest mystery, the finding of the bodies of Mr. and Mrs. John Lehrmann, an aged couple supposed to have died from gas fumes. Including this couple the total numbers fourteen.

Less than a half mile from the Lehrmann home, Peter Ross shot his wife, killing her instantly and mortally wounded his sister at the Beaulieu resort. A half mile away Winnzel E. Kabat committed the most fiendish murder ever recorded in the state and then burned the body of his victim, Michael McCarty. A young stranger was one night found murdered at a hotel roadhouse kept by a French woman Mme. Luline. His identity was never established.

A government employee was caring for the quarter boat for the winter and was murdered on the McCarty farm. Jeenie, the daughter of Charles McCarty, driving from the farm with a load of hay slipped from her seat and broke her neck. Within a quarter of a mile is the Chicago & North-Western railroad crossing, where five men have met death being struck by trains. Several persons are trying to dispose of their property and more elsewhere.

—*Eau Claire Leader*
February 15, 1907

This cursed locality has a long life span as I was contacted by current relatives who stated that the land continues to be cursed.

❖ ❖ ❖

Money Found In Haunted House

MADISON- While tearing down an old haunted house in the Sixth Ward the other evening. Daniel Trainor found an old shoe in which was hidden $1,500. The dates upon the money indicate that it had been placed there about sixteen years ago, probably by an old couple, Mr. And Mrs. Emily Behrend, both of whom died recently in Milwaukee.

—Eau Claire Leader
July 20, 1907

❖ ❖ ❖

Tips From Spirit
Set A Lunch Counter For Ghosts Every Night

MENASHA- Menasha mourns the loss of a great spiritualist, Joseph A. Sanford, aged eighty-four, a fine old wealthy Wisconsin pioneer and retired lumber dealer. He was peculiar on one point, "spiritualism." During the last ten years Mr. Sanford had not partaken of a meal or retired at night without first having the table set for the deceased members of his family.

At the retiring hour a fresh naked cake was placed on the table for the spirit members and these were consulted in all matters of importance concerning Mr. Sanford's life before any action was decided upon. It is said Mr. Sanford made lots of money from tips given him by spirits.

—Eau Claire Leader
January 1, 1908

He Talks to Ghosts
Declaration Yesterday Of Waukesha Upholsterer. Today Declared Insane By County Physician A. F. Young.

WAUKESHA- "The world is full of ghosts. I am not afraid of 'em. I like to talk to 'em. I can see and talk with the people who live in the sun, the moon, and the stars. They are disembodied spirits." August Siebner, aged 51, walked into the county jail yesterday afternoon and made this strange assertion. This morning it was ascertained that he is an upholsterer at Waukesha who had wandered away from home. Dr. A. F. Young, county physician, has pronounced him insane.

—Milwaukee Journal
January 10, 1908

The House Is Haunted
People Of Florence Are Excited Over Strange Noises

FLORENCE- A two-story dwelling house located on one of the back streets in the extreme northwestern portion of the city, which for some time past has been occupied as a residence by Mr. and Mrs. Herman Pultz, is reported to a large contingent of superstitious people during the week. All sort of strange and unexplained happenings are said to have occurred within its walls on diverse nightly occasions of late and there are not a few otherwise intelligent and sensible citizens who declare that the mysterious doings are the work of some disgruntled or grouchy "spirit." These unskeptical folk claim to have been eye-witnesses to the ghostly pranks, and of course seeing is believing. They say tables, chairs and a stove have been repeatedly overturned seemingly without human agency; and that the ghost cheerfully and correctly answers all questions propounded by the curious visitors by giving clear and distinct knocks.

Many of the people who have remained in the house throughout the night glibly relate quite a number of other interesting, though highly improbable, yarns concerning the actions of the mysterious spook. The performances, however, have evidently become a little too strenuous and realistic for the nerves of the tenants, for Mr. Plutz and wife have vacated the alleged haunted house and taken up an abode elsewhere.

The whole thing is undoubtedly the work of some of our famous Florence practical and professional jokesters, a few of whom are so clever and proficient along these lines as to carry out a scheme of this nature without the least danger of detection. Most likely the late occupants of this particular house started a report about hearing "strange noises" there, and this was a sufficient clue for the town jokesters and they laid their plan accordingly and carried them out successfully, too. The alleged haunted house, at all events, has been the sensation of the week, particularly among the denizens of the west end of the city. Certain it is, that a few jolly scamps have had no end of fun at the expense of a whole lot of nervous and superstitious people.

—*Eau Claire Leader*
January 30, 1908

The Republican Party was founded in the town of Ripon in 1854.

Ghost Story From Chippewa
Writer Sent Out Sensational To The Metropolitan Press

CHIPPEWA FALLS- Some penny-a-liner sent out the following story from Chippewa Falls regarding an apparition that is supposed to be lurking in the town of Washington:

Farmers of the town of Washington who have passed at night what is known as Lowes Creek Hill, are confident it is haunted. Frequently they have seen a specter hovering above the creek, near the hill, and repeatedly pursued by it. At times, the apparition plays jokes on the farmers by purloining some of their personal property as they pass. Usually these articles are found the next day in some out-of-the-way place. The last persons who had an experience with the "ghost" are Joseph Browning, Olwin Peloquin and Max Fredick.

—*Eau Claire Leader*
October 15, 1908

❖ ❖ ❖

Strange Happenings On Lowes Creek Hill
Was It A Ghost?

WASHINGTON- Joe Browning, Olwin Peloquin and Max Fredick, three steady young men homebound last night of street fair got along bravely until they reached Lowes Creek Hill (supposed to be haunted) and then something uncanny occurred. Something bright flashed in the trees on the creek and a curious sort of cork screw wind seemed to race around the wagon and scare the horses. Oliver's and Max's headgear was not interfered with, but strange to say Joe's nice new Christie stiff was snapped from his head and taken aloft and they could not trace it that night. It was found however, next day, and the finder brought it to the Leader office and now Mr. Browning thanks the finder very much. There have been so many things lost in and around Lowes Creek of late that if there is really a ghost there or thereabouts it would not be amiss to put "it" in connection with the Leader office in the matter of lost and found.

—*Eau Claire Leader*
October 11, 1908

Strange occurrences seem to continue to take place at Lowes Creek as I recently received a report from a woman who was driving along Lowes Creek Road when she spotted a strange woman standing on the side of the road. The woman had long dark hair and was wearing a pink night gown. The mysterious woman made no movement or reaction to the passing vehicle. The witness was too spooked to turn around and check on the woman.

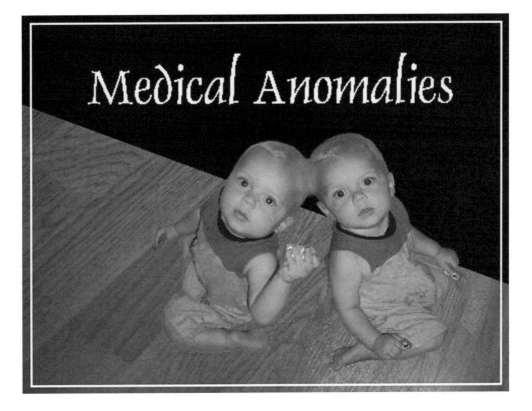

Medical Anomalies

Some joys of a traveling Salesman.

A Girl Sleeps Nearly A Week

Daughter Of Ex-Alderman Martin Of Marinette Now Wide Awake And Suffers No Ill Effects.

MARINETTE- The daughter of Edward J. Martin, an ex-alderman, awoke yesterday morning after sleeping nearly a week. During that time her slumber was wholly unbroken, and the strongest efforts of her attendants failed to awaken her She took no nourishment during that time, and the only signs of life she manifested were her breathing and a smile when attempts were made to awaken her. Thursday evening she revived and was given nourishment, but she immediately relapsed into unconsciousness, and did not awake again until yesterday morning.

Her physical condition is good and she seems to have no ill effects from her long slumber. At present she is as wide awake as ever, and knows nothing of her long sleep.

Physicians attended to her and ascribe her strange condition to a sort of nervous prostration, due in a measure to the death of her mother last summer and a fright she received about six months ago. She is 17 years old.

—*Milwaukee Journal*
January 24, 1899

CHAPTER 3 MEDICAL ANOMALIES

Turns White Again

KENOSHA- Alexander Wertenen, the tannery employee who suddenly turned black is gradually regaining his natural color. Dr. Pugh, who was called to attend him, thinks his change in color was due to chemical action. On Wednesday last Wartenen was suffering with sprained wrists. A fomentation of lead lotion was prescribed, which Wertenen used freely. Saturday he returned to his work in the tannery. In the work in which is employed a number of chemicals are used. It is likely that some of the lead lotion was absorbed, and being expelled by perspiration united with the other chemicals used in his work, forming the black pigment in the pores of his skin.

—Milwaukee Journal
February 5, 1900

❖ ❖ ❖

Girl Suddenly Blind
Miss Genevieve Jones Stricken Totally Blind While At Dinner

GREEN BAY– Miss Genevieve Jones of Oshkosh, a representative of Fleischman's yeast company, was stricken totally blind while eating dinner at the Felch hotel. The attack came without the least warning. She had a similar attack some years ago but under treatment recovered her sight. She was taken to Oshkosh.

—Milwaukee Journal
July 20, 1900

❖ ❖ ❖

Flesh Like Bone
Peculiar Condition Of Mrs. Grossman, Who Lives Near Kenosha

KENOSHA- Mrs. Frank Grossman, living near this city, is said to be affected with a peculiar malady. For some time her bones have been enlarging, until they seem to have taken place of the flesh. Every part of the body is affected and the limbs and arms of the woman seem to be as hard as the bone.

—Milwaukee Journal
June 22, 1901

Recovers His Sight

TWO RIVERS- Eight months ago Laddie Gonia, aged 18, gradually become totally blind. A prominent oculist was consulted, but failed to restore the eyesight. Recently the sight began to return slowly and he is now able to distinguish large letters. His sight is growing stronger daily.

—Milwaukee Journal
February 10, 1900

The first ice cream sundae was invented in Two Rivers in 1881.

The nation's first kindergarten class began in Watertown in 1856.

Rice Lake Man Cannot Sleep
Troubled With Strange Ailment For The Past Two Months. Consults Eau Claire Doctors.

RICE LAKE- The case of Ed Johnson of Rice Lake is puzzling the physicians of the city and a few of the Eau Claire physicians, who have been consulted in the case. The fellow with the strange ailment is a brother-in-law of J.S. Crisler, a well known citizen of Rice Lake. Mr. Johnson has not slept with the exception of a few hours, during the past two months. He is apparently in good health and has a good appetite but at night time he does not feel sleepy, in fact cannot sleep, and usually sits by the fire until a few days ago when he began to feel quite nervous and decided to consult a physician. The doctors at Rice Lake do not seem to find anything the matter with him and he came to Eau Claire recently to consult the physicians of this city. One of the citizens of Rice Lake suggests as a remedy that Johnson be placed on the police force.

—Eau Claire Leader
February 21, 1905

❖ ❖ ❖

Sight Returns Just Before Death

SHERMAN- Miss Mamie Kentbon died at the home of her niece, Mrs. Joesph Hintz, last week in the town of Sherman, with who she had made her home for the last thirty years. Twenty years ago she went bind, but almost two weeks before her death she again recovered her sight and once more beheld the surroundings amid which she lived for the last thirty years. She could easily distinguish the distant hills and the pictures, which were hung in her room. The cause of her returning eyesight is a mystery, which has been exciting much interest. Doctors are unable to explain it and many people regard it as a special act of providence.

—Eau Claire Leader
February 6, 1907

❖ ❖ ❖

Suddenly Loses Power Of Speech

RACINE- George Wright, one of the leading merchants of Racine and a lodge man of prominence, suddenly lost the power of speech and cannot utter a word. He is obliged to ask and reply to all questions in writing. Some years ago Mr. Wright was afflicted in a similar way, but recovered.

—Eau Claire Leader
December 20, 1907

❖ ❖ ❖

Knife Blade In Brain
And Man Walks A Mile To Hospital. Surgeons Have Difficulty In Extracting Knife From Joseph Sinjakovies' Skull And Pronounce His Case Most Remarkable. Has Good Chance To Recover. His Alleged Assailant Is Arrested.

MILWAUKEE- With a knife blade driven through his skull, and penetrating fully an inch into the brain. Joseph Sinjakovies walked several yards before he realized that he was severely injured. A friend with whom Sinjakovies was walking called his attention to the knife, which had penetrated the crown of Sinjakovies' hat and was sticking upright. "Perhaps I'd better hurry," said Sinjakovies. He walked a mile to the emergency hospital, where he demanded the assistance of the surprised surgeon.

The knife blade had bent in its passage through the skull, and it was extracted without difficulty by two surgeons. Sinjakovies lost consciousness at no time and talked to the surgeons and nurses about the way in which he had received his injury while the knife was being extracted. "It is a remarkable case," said Dr. Pearce. "While Sinjakovies is not out of danger, he stands a good chance of recovery. The knife entered his brain on the left side to the rear of the crown. Fortunately it missed any large blood vessels."

George Doron, an employee of the Plankinton Packing Co., was arrested at the saloon of Joseph Krippel, Twelfth St. and St. Paul Ave., as a result of the assault and was held a prisoner pending the outcome of Sinjakovies' injuries. Doran is an Austrian and Sinjakovies, a Hungarian. Sinjakovies is said to have been drinking in the saloon with Valentine Petrovies and Ivan Perie.

Doran is alleged to have insulted them. The trio finished their beer and left the saloon. As he stepped from the saloon door, Petrovies and Perie claim Doran ran after Sinjakovies and struck the knife into his head: The three friends proceeded some yards before they noticed the knife. When Sinjakovies arrived at the hospital his hat was covered with blood and his shoes were blood-soaked. Doran admitted he had struck Sinjakovies with his fist, but denied he had used a knife. Sinjakovies lost fully a pint of blood before he reached the hospital. Sinjakovies and Doran are each 20. The former is employed by the Pfister & Vogel tannery.

—Milwaukee Journal
January 1, 1906

Leg Has Been Broken Many Times Since Boyhood

RACINE- Henry Petmeir, when a boy, had his right arm broken. It was broken a second time. After he became of age he was badly hurt by a fall. Four months ago his leg was broken by a radiator falling upon it. He was albe Monday to be out on crutches for the first time. He fell and his face was cut, the leg rebroken in the same place, and the physicians say he may be crippled for life.

—Milwaukee Journal
June 12, 1901

Mysterious Creatures

Destruction Of Sheep

MISHICOT- We learn from Mr. Julins Linstedt, one of our patrons in Mishicot, that the farmers in that town have had killed within the last six weeks two hundred and twenty-six sheep, and they have thus far been unable to find out what animal is doing the mischief, as they are all killed in one manner and left without any tearing of the carcass. There are no marks of violence except a small hole behind the ears, from which the blood is sucked, and then left otherwise in perfect shape.

The farmers are alarmed, fearing their entire stock will fall victim to this strange animal, which old hunters think must be a panther; and as the "Schutzenverein" are out to a man hunting, we have every reason to believe that some of those good marksman will succeed in killing the brute, whatever it proves to be. The supervisors of the town held a meeting last Saturday, and offered a reward for the capture of the unknown animal. From the nature of the wound inflicted, we are inclined to believe it a species of bat, phyllostoma spectrum, or the vampire bat of New Spain. It is very rare, and may have escaped from some traveling menagerie.

—Waukesha Freeman
August 24, 1871

Platteville Monstrosity

PLATTEVILLE- A monstrosity in the shape of a pig came into the world last week, on Mr. Jenkyns' farm near Jenkynville, occupied by Mr. Joseph Daddow. The pig has eight legs, four ears, one eye-socket with three eye balls in it, and from the forehead a proboscis something like the trunk of an elephant.

—Janesville Gazette
April 4, 1872

A Drunken Bird

EASTON- A strange incident occurred recently in Easton which was witnessed by several persons. Some men dropped a whisky flask on a curbstone, making pieces of it. The bottle contained whisky, a small quantity of it remaining on some of the pieces. A sparrow flew down from a tree and commenced drinking the liquor. In a few minutes the bird began to stagger and could scarcely hold up its head. Presently it dropped over dead drunk. The little fellow was picked up by a peanut vendor and properly cared for. In a short time it flew away, apparently sober.

—*Milwaukee Journal*
January 17, 1880

> **Green Bay has the distinction of being Wisconsin's oldest city. It was incorporated in 1754.**

A Monstrosity

GREEN BAY- Today some boys have found the dead body of a newly born infant in a box floating down the river at the southern end of this city. The child was a monstrosity. The top of its head, from the forehead, was perfectly flat, slanting down to below the level of its ears, the latter being remarkably large. The forehead was high and bulging and the eyes set high up in it. There was no neck, the head rested directly upon the body. The body and limbs were natural and well proportioned. An official inquiry was held but nothing was elicited beyond the statement of a physician, that the infant was a full term child, born alive, and that under any circumstances it could not have lived but a few days.

—*Janesville Gazette*
March 24, 1880

Baby Monstrosity

FLORENCE- Mrs. Alonzo Morrison, of Florence, gave birth to a monstrosity in the shape of a child with four well developed legs and a duplicate set of other organs.

—*Centralia Enterprise and Tribune*
February 21, 1891

❖ ❖ ❖

Monstrosity

BEAVER FALLS- Charlie Conner, of Beaver Falls, has on exhibition a monstrosity in the shape of a chicken formed with two beaks, four legs, four wings, and three backs. It is fully developed in every respect and lived for quite a while after being hatched out. The egg from which the chicken was hatched was one of eleven places under a hen. She brought out ten chicks and then left the nest, taking her ten chickens with he and abandoning the eleventh egg. The egg was put under an old goose that was setting, but as soon as it was hatched out and the goose saw the manner of bird it was she kicked it out of the nest and it died.

—*The Daily Independent*
August 27, 1891

❖ ❖ ❖

Serpent In Red Cedar Lake

FORT ATKINSON- Red Cedar Lake near Fort Atkinson is again agitated by a monster who has lain dormant through the cold months. Several Germans were surprised while looking at what they supposed was a large stub sticking several feet above the water to see a mud turtle, which climbed upon the supposed stub to sun himself, disappear within a capacious mouth. William Ward lost five valuable sheep by the visit of the serpent. Their bodies were found in the mud partly devoured.

—*The New North*
June 9, 1892

❖ ❖ ❖

Again The Serpent

MADISON- The sea serpent was seen again by a number of young men who were out sailing on Lake Mendota. There were about twelve young men in the party and they got a good view of the creature and all of them declare that it was very large. Some say that it was fully 35 feet long, others say 30 and the lowest estimate is 25 feet. Not being on a hunt for the serpent they had no firearms and were glad to escape from the monster.

—*The New North*
November 3, 1892

❖ ❖ ❖

Find Alligator
In Black River

LA CROSSE- Yesterday while George McConnell, 1421 Avon Street, was gathering driftwood out of the Black River for his winter's woodpile he made a find that is rare in northern waters. It was nothing less than a young alligator with an extremely lively disposition.

While hauling a log ashore, McConnell noticed that it was hollow. He could have been scarcely more surprised, however, when young Mister Gator stuck his ugly snout out of the cavity. After a hard struggle, the gator was captured and is now locked up in McConnell's barn on Avon Street.

How an alligator got so far north is a matter of conjecture. Whether the one captured yesterday made his escape from some city farther north and was on his way home to the sloughs of Louisiana or whether he had wandered north in search of adventure is still a mystery.

—*La Crosse Daily Press*
October 6, 1897

Of course alligators are not native to Wisconsin and would have a hard time surviving the harsh winter cold.

Wild Man
In Chippewa Falls
Captured By A Marshall Forty Miles
North Of The City
And Now Is In Jail

CHIPPEWA FALLS- A wild man was captured in the woods forty miles north of Chippewa Falls and placed in the county jail last night. He is about seventy years of age and has lost nearly all semblance to a human being. His hair and beard are about a foot long and his clothes consist of a solitary gunny sack wrapped around his body and a pair of overalls, also a coonskin cap. Many persons went to the jail to gaze upon him.

It is impossible to hold conversation with him, as he has lost all knowledge of speech and is undoubtedly an imbecile. The strange creature wandered into Tony, on the Soo Road, and was taken in charge by the Marshall there. From appearances he has lived the life of a hermit in the wilderness for many years. He will be examined and sent to an asylum.

—*Racine Journal*
June 29, 1899

❖ ❖ ❖

Lake Mendota Sea Serpent
It Bobs Up Again To Frighten A Camping Party Of Women

MADISON– The Lake Mendota sea serpent has again appeared. It was seen this time by two women, instead of fishermen, as has always been the case in past years. Mrs. E. Grove and Mrs. J.J. Pecher and several other women who belong to the camping party on the lake saw the serpent while they were out in a boat. They saw a long, snake-like monster with a head ten inches across, and a tail which had horns. They started for shore and the serpent, apparently as much frightened as they, plunged, they say, into the depths of the lake, making a great deal of foam. The tra-

dition that there is a big sea serpent in Lake Mendota has existed for many years, and every once in a while someone is reported to have seen the monster.

—*Racine Daily Journal*
August 4, 1899

> **Lake Mendota located in Madison is touted as the most studied lake in North America. The lake covers nearly 22 miles of shoreline, is over 10,000 acres wide, and in parts the depth reaches over 80 feet.**

Farmer Shot An Alligator
Strange Game Killed In A Little Creek Near Utica.
Five-Foot Reptile Disporting Itself In Icy Wisconsin Waters.
Was Probably Released By Robert Mehlmem Two Years Ago.

UTICA- Theodore Eberts, a farmer of Utica, about eight miles west from here, has caused a sensation by shooting a five-foot alligator in the Eight-Mile Creek. Eberts was out hunting and seeing a commotion in the shallow water of the creek, he fired at it, believing it to be a big fish. To his great surprise he found that he had killed an alligator. The reptile was taken to Fisk station, where it has been viewed by scores of curious farmers, who are at a loss to account for its presence in these waters.

In this connection it is recalled that Robert Mehlman, a cigar man of this city, released a live alligator several years ago and it is suggested that it may be the same one. The Mehlman alligator when released was about three feet long and would have grown to just about the size of the one shot in Utica. By ascending Fox River and Waukau Creek it could have easily reached the spot where this one was shot.

—*Milwaukee Journal*
April 18, 1900

❖ ❖ ❖

The Half Moon Lake Alligator

OSHKOSH- Twelve years ago, people wouldn't believe there was an alligator in Half Moon Lake. We have a special from Oshkosh, dated April 18th as follows: Theodore Eberts, a farmer of Utica about eight miles west of Oshkosh, has caused a sensation by shooting an alligator 4 ½ feet long in Eight-Mile Creek. Eberts was out hunting and seeing a commotion in the shallow water of the creek, fired at it, believing it to be a big fish. To his great surprise he found that he had killed an alligator. The reptile was taken to Fisk station, where it has been viewed by scores of curious farmers, who are at a loss to account for its presence in these waters.

It is recalled that Robert Mehlman, a cigar man of this city, released a live alligator ten years ago, and it is suggested that it may be the same one. The Mehlman alligator, when released was about three feet long and would have grown to just about the size of the one shot in Utica. By ascending Fox River, and Waukau creek, it could have easily reached the spot where this one was shot.

—Eau Claire Leader
April 20, 1900

Here's A Calf That Is Bald All Over

MILWAUKEE- There is a calf on the North Side that will need the wind tempered to it if there is a cold wave. It was born three weeks ago, and it was born bald all over. It is a funny looking calf. It even hasn't any hair on its tail, and there has been much speculation as to what is the probable cause of the phenomenon. It is owned by Herman Nimmer. The mother of the calf had another calf before this one

was born. The other one was supplied with hair to the ordinary extent. They thought maybe this one would get some hair after a while, but there are no indications up to now. It is strictly bald and belongs down in the front row of calves. Mr. Nimmer is very thankful that the calf was born in the summer, else he would have had to keep it in a dry kiln to prevent freezing to death. No one seems to know why it is hairless.

—Milwaukee Journal
June 4, 1900

The dairy cow is the state's official domestic animal.

A Gigantic Tusk Found

SPRING GREEN- A valuable find was made near the home of Joseph Carbary at Spring Green, this county, recently. For several years the family had seen what was supposed to be a root of a tree sticking out of the mud in the bottom of Bear Creek. The other day while the children were playing about the creek they put a rope around the supposed root and hauled it to the shore. It proved to be a large tusk evidently of some animal that lived in these parts in the prehistoric age. It was thirty-seven inches long, twenty inches in diameter and weighed forty pounds. Mr. Carbary also secured pieces of the other tusk and is going to dig for the rest of the body.

—Milwaukee Journal
May 14, 1900

Cows Bark Like Dogs

GRANTSBURG- A peculiar disease is reported to be afflicting cattle in the northern part of Burnett County. They bark and snap like dogs.

—Milwaukee Journal
September 4, 1900

❖ ❖ ❖

Rained Horned Toads
Peculiar Phenomenon Noticed After Appleton Storm

APPLETON- A peculiar phenomenon was noticed yesterday as a result of the continued heavy rains. The showers of worms have been seen here before, but when the collection of entomological specimens which rained down from the heavens was increased by the addition of large numbers of frogs and various other insects it attracted the attention of all pedestrians. What has proved the most interesting "gift from the gods," however, was picked up today, and is an excellent specimen of a horned toad, about two-thirds grown. As the batrachian is found only in California and semi-tropical portions of the southwest, and moreover, as it was not yet fully grown, it is impossible that it could have been hatched in this climate.

—Milwaukee Journal
September 27, 1900

❖ ❖ ❖

CHAPTER 4 MYSTERIOUS CREATURES

Teamsters See Sea Lion
The Animal Was Disporting Itself In Lake About North Point.
Men Armed With Pick Axes And Clubs Went Back
But Monster Was Gone.

RACINE- Excitement ran high in the vicinity at North Point late yesterday afternoon. Rene Miller, Peter Reiplinger and a teamster named George, employees of the Reichert Construction company, were out with teams and wagons getting sand. George was quite a ways behind and had just driven down the hill as what is known as the ravine. Presently Miller and Reiplinger looked back and were startled to see the team coming on a mad gallop with the teamster wailing them with the whip and yelling at the top of his voice. He came up and almost out of breath and told of an immense fish that he saw in shallow water on the shore.

It was as long as the wagon and horses together and its tail was flapping and churning the water at a fearful rate, throwing spray into the air many feet. Miller and Reiplinger armed themselves with pickaxes and the teamster got a big club and piloted the men back to the place where he saw the fish, but the monster had got away into the deep water and no sign of it could be found. Today people have been out looking around to get a glimpse of the sea monster.

Two or three years ago it was reported that a sea monster was swimming around in this vicinity and tugs were sent out to chase and capture the creature, but it was not accomplished and it was supposed that the big serpent had sought quarters up around the north part of the lake. Mr. Miller, one of the men who went after the fish yesterday, says that according to the story told by the teamster, it was an unusually large serpent and would measure thirty feet. From the manner of the man and the way in which he told of the actions of the stranded serpent it must have been very large and of fearful strength, for the water flowed into the air in great volumes.

Where George said he saw the fish or serpent there is a sand bar, and the water is only two feet deep, but just outside it is ten feet deep and it is supposed the monster worked off this deep hole.

—*Racine Journal*
December 27, 1900

❖ ❖ ❖

Wild Man

EAU CLAIRE- Many Eau Claire women have been badly torn on barbed wire fences while climbing to get away from a half-clad "wild man" who roams the woods.

—*Marshfield Times*
July 31, 1891

❖ ❖ ❖

Sea Serpent Seen By Campers

LA CROSSE- The aged sea serpent, of whom stories are related by early pioneers of La Crosse, has again made its appearance in the vicinity of the cottage at Eagle Bluff and other places along the Mississippi River between La Crosse and Dresbach, Minnesota.

Thrilling tales are told by camping parties of hair-breadth escapes from this poisonous creature. The sea serpent was seen yesterday near Dresbach by a party of campers who landed on that side of the river to have lunch. One of the gentlemen in the party was on shore when a large snake-like creature, which had coiled around a huge log, glided off into the river, hissing like escaping steam. The serpent was greenish black in color with a few spots of white near the neck. Its head was protected by two horns, like those of a calf, and its tail lashed the water into foam before the reptile disappeared into the depths of the Mississippi. The campers did not hesitate long to seek another place for lunching.

—*La Crosse Daily Press*
July 20, 1901

According to the Wisconsin Department of Natural Resources, each year in Wisconsin more than 1.3 million fishing licenses are sold and more than 61 million fish are caught.

A Wisconsin Fish Story
Trout Which Were Frozen For Eleven Years Retain Life After Being Thawed Out

JUNCTION CITY- It is a queer fish story, that comes from Junction City, up in the central part of the state, and one that does credit even to a Wisconsin fisherman, although this is vouched for as being true. George E. Oster of Chicago is the father of the tale which tells how the writer was given some beautiful brook trout in 1873, of his placing them in an ice house, and then leaving them until 1884. At that time the ice house was destroyed by fire, and the fireman so flooded the premises, that the water formed a reservoir in the basement, where the fish were thrown out and restored to life, and where they generated 447 other fish in the ensuing three years. The very definiteness employed may be an assurance of its verity.

The very minute, 4:47 p.m. Feb. 15, 1873, is distinctly remembered as the time when the fish were deposited in the ice house. It was exactly eleven years after to a day, that the place was destroyed by fire and the fish given a fresh lease of life in the extemporized reservoir. Again, it was precisely three years later when it was decided to rebuild the ice house, leading to the discovery of the 447 young fish and the old one too. The later was easily recognized, as the writer easily remembered knocking one of the eyes out and breaking off part of its tail, while it was in a frozen condition, fourteen years previous, and these marks of identification were still prominent. Mr. Oster does not ask the public to rely entirely upon his reputation for veracity, but offers corroborative evidence in the person of Frank Blood and Arthur Sturtevant of Stevens Point, and Eugene Sheppard of Rhinelander, who, it is presumed, will substantiate the story in all its details, upon application by any doubting Thomas.

—Milwaukee Journal
March 26, 1901

❖ ❖ ❖

Saw A Wild Man
People Near Ashland Claim To Have Seen A Naked Creature Who Cannot Be Captured

ASHLAND- A wild man nearly naked and whose hands and face were covered with blood is said to have been seen near here yesterday. An undersheriff drove out to Rhoem's farm and will endeavor to capture him.

—Milwaukee Journal
April 19, 1901

❖ ❖ ❖

Alligator In Devil's Lake
Baraboo Man Claims To Have Seen Tropical Reptile

BARABOO- Emerson Loomis saw an animal about two feet long, with four legs and a long tail, near Devil's Lake. It disappeared in the lake before he could get closer. He is convinced that it is an alligator.

—Milwaukee Journal
May 20, 1901

❖ ❖ ❖

Colt Without Legs
A Freak Born Near Berlin Lacks Front Limbs

BERLIN- A freak was born on the farm of D.J. Jenne, west of Berlin, in the shape of the colt without front legs. Its hind legs are perfectly formed, but there are not even stumps where the fore legs ought to grow. The colt is full of life, and with the exception of being minus its forelegs, is fully developed and the chances are that it will live. How it will get around, however, is a hard matter to solve. It will either have to have artificial legs or be taught to jump like a kangaroo.

—Milwaukee Journal
June 12, 1901

Catch A Peculiar Fish

PORT WASHINGTON- A very peculiar fish was caught yesterday by Smith Bros, in their pound net. The fish was twenty-five inches long, not over two inches thick and shaped like a sword fish minus a sword. It has a beak like a small dirk projecting seven inches beyond the eyes and very sharp, with teeth like a trout. Local sports as well as fishermen are unable to classify the newcomer, even Fish and Game Warden Wilson admits his ignorance. The fish has been placed in the pond of G. Biederman.

—Milwaukee Journal
July 3, 1901

❖ ❖ ❖

Mind Reading Dog Will Exhibit At Y.W.C.A.

MILWAUKEE- Boz II, the mind reading dog owned by George B. Clason of Chicago, will give an exhibition of his remarkable accomplishments at the Young Women's Christian Association Friday and Saturday evenings. The dog is said to be able to do problems in arithmetic with startling rapidity. Mr. Clason is sure that it is mental telepathy. His theory is that the power is hereditary in animals and may be traced back to the Scotch shepherd dogs, who, living entirely with their masters, and not associating with other dogs, came to posses a keen sympathy.

Principals and assistant superintendents of the Chicago public schools are trying to learn if the same methods employed by Mr. Clason in teaching Boz may not be used to advantage in the instruction of children. Men will be admitted to the tests.
—*Milwaukee Journal*
February 12, 1902

❖ ❖ ❖

Battle With Eagle
Racine County Farmer In Fierce Encounter. Kills Large Bald-Headed Specimen.

RACINE- After a desperate encounter, the largest American bald eagle ever discovered in this country was killed by ex-county clerk Charles Bull near here. The bird attacked Mr. Bull in a field, badly lacerating his hands and face. It was finally dispatched by a blow on the head with his only weapon, a heavy cane. The eagle measured seventy inches from tip to tip of wings, and was evidently 15 years old.
—*Milwaukee Journal*
April 29, 1902

❖ ❖ ❖

Mongrel Chicken Terrorizes Many Women And Children

MILWAUKEE- Fighting blood is expected in game cocks, but when an old mongrel white chicken will fight anything on two legs, he is worth more than passing notice. Up on Twenty-sixth Street there is a rooster which threatens to terrorize the neighborhood as he has put all feathered stock to flight and has now turned his attention to the children and women of the vicinity.

One day last week, while the 5-year-old daughter of the family living next door to the home of the bird was out in the yard at play, she was attacked by the rooster, which perched upon her back and beat a tattoo upon her shoulders with his spurs as she ran screaming into the house. The next day the little maid's mother was passing along the rear of the house and the old bird evidently thought that his title of "cock 'o the walk" was being usurped and he made a dash to the invader. As the bird flew, the lady kicked and the ballet was a dandy while it lasted, but the lady was neither a football player nor a fancy dancer and it was only a short time until she felt her limbs tire and was obliged to seek safety in flight. There was a great crowing after this victory and yesterday the pugilistic rooster attacked the 3-year-old child of another neighbor and severely injured the child before it was rescued by its elders. The baby's face was pecked severely and her lower lip torn by the tempered fowl. There is likely to be a lynching bee on a small scale in the vicinity of Twenty-sixth Street in the near future and it will be followed by banquet, at which fricassee will be the principal dish.

—Milwaukee Journal
May 19, 1902

❖ ❖ ❖

Sheboygan Pig With Six Legs

SHEBOYGAN FALLS- On the Schwalbe farm in the town of Sheboygan Falls is a curiosity in the form of a pig with six legs. The animal is seven years old and is very healthy and strong. The additional legs have their beginning at about what would be the elbows of the fore legs. The small porker is very agile using the six feet with the most remarkable dexterity.

—Milwaukee Journal
August 22, 1901

❖ ❖ ❖

Takes Curious Fish Out Of The Lake

RACINE– William Wuertzberger dipped a curious fish out of Lake Michigan. It has the head of a lizard and body of a fish, is

fourteen inches long and two-and-a-half inches in diameter, of grayish color and with black spots. It has four feet, resembling those of a lizard, but much smaller and the tail of an eel. When placed in the water with other fish it emitted pills which dissolved and killed the other fish. There were no eyes. There are two small ears, an eighth of an inch in diameter, but when the fish became angry would extend over an inch.

—Milwaukee Journal
July 10, 1902

Wisconsin is home to 14,927 lakes which is more than the 11,842 lakes in the neighboring state of Minnesota which is known as the "Land of 10,000 Lakes."

Two-Headed Calf Is A La Crosse Monstrosity

LA CROSSE- John Desmond owns a two-headed calf. The animal has two complete heads and is several weeks old. It is apparently in the best of health.

—Milwaukee Journal
August 6, 1902

❖ ❖ ❖

Sea Serpent Time

NEENAH- With a five-legged frog at Kaukauna, captured at Brighton Beach, and a double-headed snake at Appleton, caught at Stroebe's island, and a hydra-headed politician on exhibit at Oshkosh, it is about time Neenah secured that sea serpent claimed to have been seen off the point on Sunday last night. Don't be a clam.

—*Janesville Daily Gazette*
August 19, 1902

❖ ❖ ❖

Finds Strange Animal
La Crosse Man Finds Nest Of Unknown Species In Well. Shape Of Animal Resembles A Miniature Hippopotamus With Legs Cut Off Near The Body.

LA CROSSE- Bert Student, employed by Thill & Lapitz of this city, yesterday ran onto a nest of animals, the name of which no local student of the animal science has yet been able to tell. The animals were found down a well which he was repairing. The premises are in the eastern portion of the city. When he took the boards off the top he noticed a strange animal clinging to the pump. He promptly knocked it off. When he discovered others, his curiosity becoming aroused. He captured one and put it in alcohol.

The specimen captured is about three or four inches long, cream color with black markings about a quarter of an inch long all over the body. In shape the animal resembles a miniature hippopotamus with its legs sawed off close to the body. From the large mouth two forks of a spindle tongue protrude and with this the animal feels its way about. It has no eyes at all, indicating that it is a species that lives in caves or other dark places. It is of a consistency very clammy and damp. Just what the animal is and how it got there is a mystery, for it is evidently miles from its regular place.

There has always been a mystery connected with the well where the animals were found. There can be felt at times on hot days, gusts of fresh, cold air which evidently come from the interior of the earth. The air is damp and there is a sound of running water heard through the loose sand at the bottom. It is in the populous eastern portion of the town.

—*Grand Rapids Tribune*
September 10, 1902

> **In 1900, the population of Wisconsin was just over 2 million. Today nearly 5 ½ million people call the state home.**

Put In Lock-Up

JANESVILLE- One of the freaks which was offered for public gaze upon the payment of a small admission fee was a "half-man-half-woman" which was very popular at the onset of the week. Unfortunately, a part of the proceeds which were taken in were used by the freak for firewater and the man half of it became uproariously drunk, creating such a disturbance that the police transferred it to the calaboose. The monstrosity will not be put on exhibition again.

—*Janesville Daily Gazette*
September 25, 1902

❖ ❖ ❖

Found A Monstrosity

LINCOLN- One of the most remarkable natural curiosities ever discovered in this country was unearthed in the town of Lincoln this week, and will be exhibited here during the carnival. The anomalous animal is a cross between a sheep and a hog, showing some of the characteristics of each, and has been named by the present owners a Schef-Schwein. The curiosity was raised by John Anderson on his farm six miles west of the city and is a year old.

It resembles a sheep more than a hog in build, but it is much larger than the ordinary sheep, weighing about 300 pounds. The animal is healthy and lively, has the body of a sheep and the head and limbs of a hog and grunts like a hog, though, covered with a heavy coat of wool. The Schef-Schwein is now in the hands of a Marshfield syndicate and will be exhibited in a tent as one of the star attractions of the fair. Don't wait to see it.

—*Marshfield Times*
September 26, 1902

❖ ❖ ❖

Lake Geneva Sea Serpent

LAKE GENEVA- A sea serpent sixty-five feet long and from eight to ten inches in diameter was reported at Lake Geneva.

—*Janesville Gazette*
September 29, 1902

❖ ❖ ❖

Sea Serpent

LAKE GENEVA- There is no need of assurance that the Lake Geneva sea serpent is not an ordinary water snake. It is generally known that cold water can conjure no such visions in the brain of those who prefer it to be manufactured tipples.

—*Janesville Daily Gazette*
October 1, 1902

❖ ❖ ❖

Alligator In The Rock River
It Was Shot By A Spring Brook Young Man On Saturday

SPRING BROOK- While Will and George Berger were playing alongside the river at Spring Brook Saturday afternoon they saw a strange looking creature that resembled a lizard crawl out of the water and onto a log. Frightened they ran to their home and informed their brother, Otto Berger, of what they had seen. He immediately secured his rifle and accompanied them back to the spot where the creature had been seen.

The "big lizard" was still sunning itself in the log and Mr. Berger took careful aim and fired, striking him just behind the ear. When recovered from the water it was found to be an alligator nearly three feet in length. One of the legs of the "gator" was missing but otherwise he was a fine specimen. Many called at the Berger residence, No 2 Eastern Avenue, yesterday to see the curiosity. No one has been able to offer any adequate explanation of his presence in the waters of the Rock River.

—*Janesville Daily Gazette*
September 21, 1903

❖ ❖ ❖

Who Said He Saw A Sea Serpent?
Starr And Fathers Both Deny Imputation.
Now Up To County.

DELAVAN LAKE- The Delavan Lake sea serpent has again been seen, or at least it was "something big." It was three gentlemen from Janesville, who are in camp at the assembly, who only the strictest of temperance principles prevail and one of the three is the county clerk of Rock County, and the three each and severally, upon one solemnly affirm that they saw in the lake the head of some large animal or fish protruding some two feet from the water and moving in an unexplainable fashion.

The neck was at least twelve inches in circumference and the head was simply enormous. The creature disappeared upon their approach and they have since been discussing its identity. Some aver that it is the sea serpent others that it is a big pickerel and others have different theories, but Nev. Washburn, who is authority of such matters, says that it is a deep sea porpoise which he brought from the Gulf of Mexico.

The above is an extract from the *Chicago Chronicle* for yesterday. The county clerk of Rock County is Frank P. Starr, so he was called to account. "Not guilty," said Mr. Starr, "I haven't been near Delavan Lake. Perhaps it is Jim Fathers. They may have confused the county clerk with the city treasurer." Mr. Fathers was next accosted, "Not guilty," was his story. "I was at the assembly, but I didn't see the serpent, or start the report. I'll tell you who it must be. It was Miles Rice. It was the county treasurer and not the county clerk." Mr. Rice is out of the city and will not be here until Thursday. In the meantime the county treasurer's reputation for veracity rests under a heavy cloud and his return is eagerly awaited.

—*Janesville Daily Gazette*
August 3, 1903

❖ ❖ ❖

Greatest Freak Ever

UNITY- Without a doubt the greatest freak ever produced in Wisconsin's animal kingdom came to light last Friday in the town of Unity, Clark County, when a Shropshire cow owned by Wm. Blinning gave birth to a monstrosity in the shape of an eight legged lamb that will be a money maker. The animal has two bodies, eight legs and only one head, all fully developed. The head is normal except there is an extra pair of ears attached to the back of the head. It died shortly after birth and is now in the hands of O.H. Heinz, a taxidermist, who will mount it.

—Wisconsin Valley Leader
May 3, 1906

Monster Black Snake
Disturbing Peace Of Residents On Water Street.
Is Six Feet Long.

EAU CLAIRE- Snakes are found in many other places besides Water Street, but large snakes and black snakes as large, black and intelligent as the particular individual which hangs out in the neighborhood of No. 6 fire hall, are uncommon reptiles.

Several residents who have caught sight of him say he must be at least six feet in length. His mouth is as wide as a crocodile's, body the size of a kangaroo. The big fellow is almost wise enough to talk and has conversed several times with West Side policemen who, of course, talk only

in the language of the club.

Monday morning this descendent of Edan's confusion was caught lounging on the sidewalk right in from of the Water Street fire hall and did not seem to be alarmed about it either, until one of the boys, Jim Weiss, we think his name is, ran at him with a piece of hose, but the reptile was too smart for him. He jumped through the rubber cylinder and escaped before Jim had time to turn around.

Several ladies of the West Side have also seen him on many occasions. One time the wary charmer was discovered climbing a telegraph pole to attack the beautiful bird house which the boys have built for the home of martens and other birds of paradise. Quite a number of the snakes have been killed this spring in various localities on the West Side, too, but the king of reptiles is still at large. If he is not captured within the next few days, the vigilant committee appointed to preserve order will play their last trump card. They will send for ex-alderman Martin Page, the hero of volumes of snake stories and other cheerful brevities. Mr. Pages' experiences in woodcraft has brought him in contact with many species of snakes, so the fate of the Water Street monster will be left to him. Martin is out of town present, but may arrive at any moment.

—Eau Claire Leader
October 4, 1906

❖ ❖ ❖

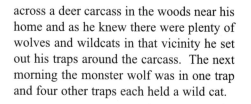
Chicken
Has Human Face

PRESTON- A chicken with a human face is attracting attention in Preston. It was secured by Edward Johnson from a flock in this vicinity. The fowl is a year old, and had attracted no attention until it appeared sick, when its owner discovered the wonderful likeness.

The hen has no bill whatever, but in its place is a perfectly formed nose. Beneath the nostrils is a mouth and chin, but in place the feathers lay parted and perfectly smooth. The cheeks are puffy, but rosily red. The hen was purchased by Mr. Johnson who sent it to a taxidermist in Chicago, where it was mounted. He has received an offer of $50 for the freak, but declines it.

—*Eau Claire Leader*
January 12, 1908

❖ ❖ ❖

Wolf
Over Six Feet In Length
Captured By Henry Walter In Ruby.
Also Traps Four Wild Cats.

RUBY- One of the largest wolves killed in Chippewa County was laid low a few days ago by Henry Walter in the town of Ruby. Henry Walter was in the city yesterday afternoon to receive the bounty from County Treasurer Cameron and he stated that the wolf measured six feet four inches from tip to tip and weighed about 150 pounds. The scalp which he exhibited was enormous. Mr. Walter says that he came

across a deer carcass in the woods near his home and as he knew there were plenty of wolves and wildcats in that vicinity he set out his traps around the carcass. The next morning the monster wolf was in one trap and four other traps each held a wild cat.

Mr. Walter brought the wolf scalp and the scalps of the wild cats to the courthouse and received $22 in bounties from the county. He will receive an equal amount from the state, making a total of $44.

—*Eau Claire Leader*
March 13, 1908

❖ ❖ ❖

Beast Causes Terror

EAU CLAIRE- A wild beast said to be a panther has been terrorizing residents in the southwestern part of Eau Claire County and the northeastern portion of Pepin County. Some of the farmers, upon waking up mornings, find that some of their sheep and young stocks and calves have been devoured. A farmer's son was followed for a short distance.

—*La Crosse Tribune*
March 19, 1908

❖ ❖ ❖

Catches Sword Fish In
Eau Claire River
Local Angler Makes Rare Catch
Last Evening

EAU CLAIRE- James J. Raymond brought to the *Leader* office last evening a sword fish, which he caught below the Eau

Claire River dam at the Linen Mill. It measured about three feet in length, and had a sword a little more than six inches long and when opened spread across a space of five inches.

This is a rare catch in this part of the country. The fish is a salt water specimen and very seldom seen in fresh water streams. How it comes to be in these waters is a mystery. Mr. Raymond was fishing with the ordinary tackle and was quite surprised with his find. The fish still showed signs of life when exhibited at the Leader office last evening.

—*Eau Claire Leader*
June 18, 1908

❖ ❖ ❖

Discover Strange Fish In The River

Head Like A Bass, Body Like A Pike. Esch Will Investigate. Communicate With Authorities At Washington To Learn Identity Of Freak.

LA CROSSE- A very queer unnamed fish has been seen by the fishery crew this season. It is a fish that has never been seen in the Black River before and experts do not know what to call it. The odd fish has a mouth like a bass and is shaped like a pike. Its color is changeable according to the weather and at this time of the year is mud black. Mr. Desmond has a minnow of this odd fish and it lies in the bottom of the bowl never moving its fins. If disturbed by touch it will dive, jump out of the water

and still up all the dirt that it can and then return to the bottom of the bowl. Congressman Esch will probably make inquires with the experts at Washington as to the identity of the fish.

—*La Crosse Tribune*
November 14, 1908

At 215 square miles, Lake Winnebago is Wisconsin's largest lake.

Freak Fish Is Snared

EAU CLAIRE- What may be termed a "chameleon fish" has been discovered by the government seiners working in the Black and Mississippi Rivers near here, and so far local scientists, who have been trying to establish the identity of the freak, have failed. The fish differs in many particulars from the usual fish both in habits and in looks. During the time it has been in the hands of the local fishery crew it has changed in hue several times, each variation coming with a drop or rise in temperature.

With the recent cold spell that invaded this part of the state it shifted from a light "pike color" to a dark, almost the color of a channel catfish. With the head of a black bass it has the body of a sand pike. The head tallies with that of a bass with the exception of the red mark in the eye, characteristic of the black bass. The body, shaped like a pike has none of the pike's

characteristic colorings. When startled by a touch, instead of darting forward, or to the side, as do most fish, it dives to the bottom of the tank and with a few flips of its tail stirs up the sediment, completely enveloping itself in the cloud. It rarely swims forward, but down and over, practically "looping the loop."

The attention of Congressman Esch has been called to the freak and he is in communication with the United States Fish Commission in an effort to establish its identity.

—*Eau Claire Leader*
January 6, 1909

❖ ❖ ❖

Big Fish Visits Racine
Residents See Monster Sturgeon Swimming Along Shores Of Lake. Said To Weigh One Hundred Pounds.

RACINE- The residents along the lake shore are telling of a monster fish, supposed to be a sturgeon, which has been seen upon several occasions swimming in the waters of the lake. According to reports, the fish is four to six feet in length and weighs at least 100 pounds. Those who have seen it, declare it is the largest ever seen in these parts. Bathers on the beach have been warned to keep away from the mighty monster of the deep.

It is thought that the fish came from the northern part of the lake, where the species is found. Fishermen are afraid to try to catch the swimmer because the local nets are not of sufficient strength to endure the strains of a fight with a fish of such ponderous proportions.

—Racine Daily Journal
July 12, 1909

> **The current record for the largest Lake Sturgeon caught in Wisconsin is 6 feet 5 inches. It was caught in 1979 on Yellow Lake in Burnett County.**

And This Is A Real Fish Story

Five-Pound Bass Leaps A Suicidal Episode. It Happened At Lake Hallie And Is Told By Descendants Of Geo. Washington.

LAKE HALLIE- What do you know about that? A five-pound bass voluntarily jumps into a boat at Lake Hallie, and allows itself to be caught! Sounds odd, doesn't it? But it's gospel truth. Monday evening, while Charles W. Lincoln, a barber at 614 Water Street, was rowing with a friend, this eccentric five-pound bass unpremeditatingly committed suicide.

Mr. Lincoln had been quietly rowing along, neither he nor his friend were talking. Everything was still. Suddenly, a splash and a bang startled the rowers. Mr. Lincoln quickly looked around and saw the fish struggling under the seat in the front end of the boat. After a tussle he captured it, and brought it to shore.

A great number of people at Electric Park examined the fish and were interested by the story. Now, this may sound rather like a modern day fish fact, but ask any real enthusiast, ask any old hunter and fisher who frequents the northern woods for big game, and they will tell you that fish, at night time often jump into boats! The fish are attracted by some glittering object, a jeweled pin, a silver cigar case, a pair of gold rimmed glasses, or a sparkling diamond ring. There's the proof, and we positively believe in Mr. Lincoln's story.

—Eau Claire Leader
September 8, 1909

❖ ❖ ❖

Wild Man Seen In Hewitt

Marshy Thicket Haunted By Nearly Nude Man. Evidently Insane. Seen By Several People But Runs Like A Deer When Approached.

HEWITT- The appearance of the so-called "wild man" who is thought to inhabit a wooded spot near the old Geo. Zollinger place about a mile east of Hewitt, has caused considerable excitement here the past week. The man is a wild, unkempt specimen, habited only in a shirt, more abbreviated than a Scotch kilt costume, and wild as a hawk in his actions.

He has been seen by several people in broad daylight and the story is neither a hoax nor an hallucination. Mr. and Mrs. C. Echwell, who reside near the place where the freak is supposed to lie concealed, which is a dense thicket on low ground, have seen him several times. When he sights a person or any attempt is made to approach him, the wild man runs for his lair with the speed of a deer. He puts one hand on a fence post and vaults a five wire fence as easily as a college athlete, and his speed defies pursuit.

Officers Schmitt and Thompson of this city, and Sheriff Griffin of Grand Rapids, have all been over the ground but have not yet seen the apparition. They are specially anxious to catch him this week in order that he may be used as a star attraction at the street fair next week. The report that the capture had been made by Griffin and Schmitt last week was a mistake, the result of a joke perpetrated on a salon keeper by the officers, with the aid of Curly Babcook, who personated the wild man in realistic style.

—*The Marshfield Times*
August 17, 1910

❖ ❖ ❖

Chick Has Three Legs In Good Working Order

EAU CLAIRE- Great is the excitement on the North Side these days. When P.T. Barnum traveled around the world with a circus full of all manner of freaks from a stuffed mermaid to a goat with the tincaneatis, he did not believe the day would come when Mrs. Anna Schwartz, a widow, living at 1304 Richards Street this city, would be exhibiting a three-legged chicken.

Looks like a mix between a bantam and an absinthe frappe, said one of the admiring throng yesterday, as they gathered about in the rear yard of Mrs. Schwartz's home and gazed in wonder at the freak, each one with a theory to advance, but the three-legged chicken strutted about the crowd with utter disdain. Its three perfect legs work progressively thus adding materially to its pedestrian capacity. "It's a rooster chicken, too," said the small boy, this intelligence bursting upon him when the three legged freak tossed back its head and crowed in a most alarming manner. The chicken's modus operandi does not differ from that of the other members of the flock, except that one foot follows the other progressively back and forth, the extra leg growing out between the two. Mrs. Schwartz is quite proud of her new possession, and it has become the object of joy and envy to every small boy in the entire neighborhood.

It is on exhibition at any and all times and the owner is very glad to display it for the amusement of those who wish to get a glimpse of the freak. B.A. Giese, Mrs. Schwartz's son-in-law, who lives next door, has become press agent for the fowl, and never tires of telling of its wondrous performance. When the chicken struts around the yard it affords infinite amusement to the youngsters and the adults stand by and try to figure it out. The chicken arrived one day with a dozen other chicks over the same route. It kicked and pecked

its way through the shell and after its tiny eyes had ceased blinking, and becoming accustomed to the daylight, it lifted its tiny wings, stretched forth three perfect chicken legs, uttered a tiny squeak, and from then on proceeded to grow and develop in a most satisfying manner.

—Eau Claire Leader
September 9, 1909

❖❖❖

Alligator In Badger Lake

OSHKOSH- This morning in Lake Winnebago, south of Oshkosh, one of the leading fisherman, G. W. Ferandez, got an alligator of good size about thirty feet from shore. He was unable to account for the strange visitor, which is usually found in southern waters.

—Eau Claire Leader
July 30, 1910

❖❖❖

Saw Monster Alligator

CLINTONVILLE- "The presence of my husband and brother-in-law and two other men is probably all that prevented my niece Selma Schauder, and I from almost dying from fright last Thursday afternoon when we discovered an immense alligator swimming toward us with his mouth open and making a savage hissing noise," said Mrs. H. Peterson of Chicago, in referring to the report that she had seen a live alligator in Grass Lake, near the city. "Mr. Peterson and my brother-in-law, William Schauder, city treasurer of Clintonville, were fishing in the weeds along Gibson's island, across the neck of the lake from our cottage, and Selma and I started out in another rowboat to join them. I was just learning to row and was going slowly. The men came out of the weeds just before he got there and the first thing I knew I heard Selma, my little niece, scream. I looked around and saw an alligator about six feet long swimming on top of the water towards us. It was only about six feet from us when I dropped my oars and began screaming for help. "The men were only about twenty feet away and came up as rapidly as possible. Just as Mr. Peterson raised his oar to strike the alligator over the head, it dived into the water and escaped into the weeds." Mr. Peterson and Mr. Schauder, as well as two men from Chicago, who are camping on Pine Lake, and who were also near at the time, corroborates Mrs. Peterson's account of the incident, and all agree that the alligator was at least six feel long, that its head was about a foot long, its eyes as large as those of a cow.

The campers and resorters, especially those from Chicago and Milwaukee are excited over the discovery of a hungry alligator in the Clover Leaf Lakes, and from fishing and boating the pastime has now changed to hunting for the alligator. Although many scoff at the idea of an alligator being able to live in the waters of a Wisconsin lake, no one is able to tell what else it was that was seen by at least a dozen people in the last three days. Some say it might have been a large mud turtle, or a sturgeon, or pickerel, but none of them answer to the descriptions given by those who have seen it. About thirteen years ago a friend in the south sent an alligator about eighteen or twenty inches long to Richard Jackson, a restaurant keeper in the city. Twelve years ago Mr. Jackson gave the alligator to A.C. McComb, the Oshkosh timber and real estate dealer, who built the resort on Pine Lake, one of the three lakes in the group known as Clover Leaf Lakes, and Mr. McCombs, after keeping it for several weeks in a little pond, threw it into the lake and since then it has not been seen.

—*Eau Claire Leader*
August 30, 1910

❖ ❖ ❖

Waupaca County's Sea Serpent Story
Strange "Beastie" That Crawls Or Swims, With Huge Paws And Frightens People

CLINTONVILLE- Waupaca County and its Clover Leaf Lakes have a sea serpent story. Eight reputable residents have seen the monster. As a result, terror reigns among the Milwaukee and Chicago people who have cottages along the lakes. As described by those who have seen the thing, it is more than six feet long, can swim on the surface or crawl about on the bottom. Its feet have long claws. Last

CHAPTER 4 MYSTERIOUS CREATURES

Thursday it chased two women in a boat. William A. Schrander, city treasurer of Clintonville, has seen the thing also. A baby alligator was turned loose in the lakes some years ago and the supposed sea serpent may be this reptile.

—*Janesville Daily Gazette*
August 22, 1910

❖ ❖ ❖

Maine Strangeness

MAINE- Frank Morrow, town of Maine, this county has a freak animal combining the characteristics of the cat and the rabbit, the head belongs to that of a cat, the body like that of a rabbit.

—*Marshfield Times*
September 7, 1910

Columbia County Eruption

SPRINGVALE- S.B. Hallock, of Springvale, informs us of a letter of a strange phenomenon which occurred on his farm on that town, last year. A violent eruption of the earth occurred, throwing up a mass of earth two feet square and four feet in length. About a rod from the place flashes of light have been observed frequently for the past fifteen or sixteen years.

Mr. H. has broken up the ground where the eruption occurred, and in crossing the place he plowed up a number of pieces of what he was informed was stone-coal, a sample of which he has sent us. We have forwarded it to Madison for the opinion of scientific men there. We have heard stories before similar to what Mr. Hallock writes us, and we think it a case which should be investigated.

—*Janesville Gazette*
March 2, 1871

❖ ❖ ❖

The Skeleton Sharps
**More Excavations In
The vicinity Of Milton.
Several Mounds Opened And
Their Contents Examined.
Further Evidence That The Indians
Were Not The Original Possessors
Of America.**

MILTON- Mr. W. P. Clarke, of Milton, with a party composed of the Lapham Archaeological Society, of Milwaukee, Mr. E. S. Bailey A.B. of the Hahnemann Medical College of Chicago, and several of the Milton College students, visited the mound region on the west bank of Koshkonong, this week. Laborers had excavated five mounds to the level where the remains were supposed to lay, previous to their visit, consequently only a small quantity of soil had to be removed before laying bare the remains of the ancient individuals, whose bones until now, lain undisturbed for centuries.

The first mound opened was seventy feet in diameter, and ten feet in depth. The top soil in all the mounds was similar to that found in the vicinity, but the remaining layers were very diffierent from that usually found in that region, and were brought there by artificial means beyond a shadow of a doubt, and were probably taken from the lake shore, as muscle shells were found from below the natural layer of soil, clean down to the bottom. The skeletons were found resting upon the yellow sand ten feet below the surface, and immediately above the usual ashy substance composed chiefly of lime. From this mound twelve skeletons were removed, mostly in badly broken condition, the bones showing great antiquity, still some of the larger bones were in a fair state of preservation. Two skulls were removed in good order, the most perfect in fact that have ever been secured in this region and several upper jaws containing teeth well preserved.

The next mound was seventy-five feet in diameter and was at least twelve feet in depth. There was nothing new developed in this excavation, it being similar to the one first opened. Three smaller mounds were excavated, and in one of these was found something never before exhumed in this section. Near the head was found a large number of pieces of pottery, and with them a very large shell and also the upper shell of a turtle. These were evidently ornaments and had been placed in the piece of pottery and buried with the "big injun."

The pottery will be patched up, and an idea can them be gained of its shape. It is the first pottery ever discovered in any of the mounds in that locality Not a single bone or flint implement was found in any of the mounds, while in the one opened last fall a large number were exhumed. Among the bones exhumed were some that are of special interest to the students of anatomy, and those savants who make the study of prehistoric man a special feature. Four of the upper bones of the arm's humerus were secured in a good state of preservation, and had the peculiar perforation at the lower end, found only in the gorilla and the lowest order of the human family.

This peculiar formation consists of a perforation at the lower end of the humerus about one-eighth of an inch in diameter, and is not found in the antimony of any civilized race or the Indian tribes of the present age. In the top of the mound from which these remains were taken, at a depth of two feet, the skeleton of an Indian was removed, but the humerus showed no perforation, and, in fact, the conformation would not admit of its being found, the one being as thick at that particular point as it is in the humerus of civilized men. This is conclusive evidence that the race interred in these mounds are a distinct race from the Indians now inhabiting this country, and, in fact shows that they are an extinct race of people. Prof. Bailey has been presented with a humerus having this peculiar perforation, and will place it in the anatomical department of the Hahnemann Medical College, where Chicago savants can examine its peculiarities and deduce their own conclusions as to the truth of our position. Further resources will be presented in this great graveyard of an extinct race next spring, under the direction of Mr. Clark, of Milton, and new developments will probably be made.

—*Janesville Gazette*
September 29, 1877

The entire city of Alma is listed on the National Register of Historic Places.

Toads Tumble From Sky

LA CROSSE- During the heavy shower yesterday afternoon an exceedingly large number of small but exceedingly active toads put in an appearance, in many places almost covering the ground and sidewalks. They were most numerous about the depot at 2nd and Vine Streets, where they excited much wonder among the Milwaukee & St. Paul Railroad employees.

The important question is, of course, "Where did the toads come from?" Captain Moulton, being placed upon the rack by a reporter, duly testified and said that he was on a platform adjoining the depot and saw the toads fall from the sky. Not only did he see them as they struck the platform, but also saw them in the air before they reached the end of their aerial flight. This is good testimony and we submit it.

—*La Crosse Republican*
July 12, 1878

❖ ❖ ❖

A Legend Of Lake Koshkonong

EDGERTON- Many of the guests of Koshkonong Hotel, kept by the genial landlord, Robt. Carr, Esq., have viewed the large Indian mound situated about forty rods southeast of the hotel, in a piece of second growth timber, and looked with curiosity upon the various other mounds in that locality, yet but few persons have heard the story of the origin of these works of a prehistoric race.

While stopping for a few days lately at the above hotel, during an afternoon ramble the writer met an old Indian on the shore of the lake near the foot of the bank upon which the large mound is located. His lodge was made under the spreading branches of a willow tree near a spring of clear, cold water; with him were his two sons, both very old men. The Ancient Indian has made periodical visits to this spot from a time beyond which the memory of no white man runneth back. This relic of a past century repeated to me, in broken English, the following "Legend of Lake Koshkonong."

CHAPTER 5 ODDITIES

There dwelt, many years ago, on the banks of the lake at this place Ko-Ka-Mo, an Indian Chief, and his family consisting of his wife, two sons, and a daughter. The latter La-Lu-Ma, was known far and wide for her great personal beauty and rare accomplishments. Her form was as lithe and yet as sinewy as the antelope's. With large expressive eyes whose luster rivaled the stars; a rich-hued transparent skin through which the red blood could be seen when she blushed at some gallant remark of a warrior; and with her long, glossy, black hair braided down her back or twined about her head, with here and there a white flower entwined in its folds, she was the admired of all the young men of her tribe, and also of those of other tribes who were so fortunate as to have seen her.

None could manage a canoe more skillfully, or shoot an arrow with more success than she; and many a trophy from the water and the forest added to the family larder, attested her proficiency in the hunt. Scattered about on both sides of the river which at this point flows out of from the lake, were the numerous lodges of the tribe. The Wigwams of the chief and his household were built on the limestone bluff just east of where the boat house of the hotel is now seen. Owing to the perceptions formation of the rocks composing the walls of this headland an approach from the lake to the chief's habitation was considered out of the question, and the land approach being at night always guarded by trusty sentinels it was deemed impossible for an enemy to gain access to the headquarters of the chief.

Across the bay to the north, about a mile, on a point of land, there lived a famous young warrior, called by his tribe Ter-Kum-Ska (the brave hearted.) His tribe, which was not on friendly terms with that to which La-Lu-Ma belonged, and Ko-Ka-Mo saw with anger that Ter-Kum-Ska was paying court to his daughter. No hostile act had ever occurred between the two tribes, but Ko-Ka-Mo forbade his daughter receiving attentions from this warrior of an unfriendly tribe, and ordered his own warriors who were on guard at his family wigwams, to shoot the objective able suitor if found near the forbidden spot. But many were the times on dark and stormy nights when Ter-Kum-Ska scaled the limestone bluff and met the fair Indian maiden on its supposed inaccessible banks; for, notwithstanding her father's stern refusal to admit her lover to her presence, the girl loved the dusky warrior, and, loving him truly, ran the risk of the clandestine meetings. But there came a fatal time at last.

It was a wild, boisterous night. A northeast gale swept the lake and the waters lashed with fury the rocks at the base of the old cliff. The trees in the brow of the bluff swayed and bowed to the blast at which roared through the forest beyond. Yet as such a time as this the fearless lover crossed the stormy bay and landed in safety at the foot of the perpendicular chasm up through which he had often climbed. By means of his light canoe placed upright against the rock he gained a foothold in the crevices in the upper portion of the cliff, and quickly gained the summit. For a moment he stood beneath a tree awaiting the appearance of La-Lu-Ma, to whom he had given a signal, announcing his arrival.

Often she has been clasped to his manly breast on this spot; often here their vows of constancy had been exchanged; but this was to be their last meeting. The faithful maiden heard the call, and had nearly reached the trysting spot when she discovered her father in the act of drawing his bow upon her unsuspecting lover. With a bound like the wild gazelle she sprang to shield the form of the one she loved so well from the weapon of an angry parent. The next instant the bowstring twanged, and the flint-tipped arrow pierced through the hearts of the lovers and transfixed their forms to the tree.

United in life, they were not separated in death. The accidental killing of his daughter crushed the old chief to the earth. The large mound was raised over the remains of La-Lu-Ma by her chieftain father who gathered all his tribe to erect the monument. He also caused other mounds in her honor to be built near. Some of these have the forms of various animals. Having performed this duty, the old chief died of a broken heart and was buried beneath a conical mound near his unfortunate daughter.

Another mound near covers the body of his wife. Although untold ages have passed away since these events occurred, the monuments are still distinctly visible, and by means of a boat the visitor can reach the base of the limestone cliff and see the perpendicular fissure in the rock where, hidden from view from either side, the bold Indian lover, centuries ago, scaled the supposed inaccessible bank to meet the beautiful and faithful La-Lu-Ma, who lost her life in the vain endeavor to save his.

—*Edgerton Reporter*
August 28, 1885

❖ ❖ ❖

Dancing Ball Of Fire Frightens Girls

LA CROSSE- About 7:30 last evening the dining room girls at the Hotel Law, 124 S. 2nd Street, received a bad fright. They were standing in the hotel dining room when they claim they saw a ball of fire, about the size of a man's head, come dancing through the air toward the hotel. It entered an open window and after playing about the ceiling for a few moments suddenly flashed and disappeared.

The girls were badly frightened and lost no time in getting out of the room. A traveling man who was eating his supper at the time saw the flash of light but did not see the ball. He supposed it to be a flash of lightning. If the ball was not a product of the girls' imagination, it was probably what is commonly known as will-o'-the-wisp, or *ignis fatuus*.

—*La Crosse Republican Leader*
June 21, 1893

Escaped Being Buried Alive

Door County Villagers Have A Great Sensation.
Supposed Corpse Comes To Life While Being Prepared For The Grave.
Tries To Escape From The House But Is Detained.
Was Conscious During The Terrible Ordeal.

NASEWAUPEE- A remarkable escape from being buried alive happened in the town of Nasewaupee. Jacob Groth, son of Chas Groth, had been ill for some time and on the night in question he died to all appearances. The boy was laid out and neighbors came to the home of the deceased to keep night watch. Just before consigning the remains to the coffin, and before dressing it preparatory thereto, it was deemed advisable to wash the "corpse."

While performing this act the supposed dead boy sprang up from the cooling board to the astonishment of all present, and made an effort to escape from the house. So terribly frightened was everybody that this was nearly accomplished before the assembled persons had recovered their senses. When the boy was caught he was partly out of his head, and it was feared he would lose his reason from the terrible strain.

He says he could hear everything that was going on around him, and realized the terrible predicament he was in. It was the fear of being buried alive that caused him to try and escape when he came out of his trance of forty-eight hours. His recovery is very doubtful.

—Janesville Daily Gazette
January 20, 1899

Door County has more lighthouses (10), miles of shoreline (250), and more state parks (5) than any other county in the United States.

Giant Indian Bones
Discovery Of An Extraordinary Skeleton Near Fond du Lac

SAINT CLOUD- An Indian skeleton was dug up on the farm of Matt and Joseph Leon, one mile south of St. Cloud, Sunday. There is nothing strange in finding an Indian skeleton, but this one was a giant in size, his frame measuring seven feet. He must have been a man of note among his people, for he was buried in a large mound, sixteen handsome arrows surrounding the body.

The skull was brought to this city and is on exhibition in one of the Main Street windows. Near the Huber gravel pit skeletons by the hundreds have been dug up for the past several years. Most of the bodies are in a sitting position, with the face towards the east, to face the rising sun.

—*Centralia Enterprise and Tribune*
June 10, 1899

❖ ❖ ❖

A Doomed Car
Electric Car No. 16 Which Has Killed Four People Taken Out Of Service And Laid Up

RACINE- The *Milwaukee Sentinel* of this morning publishes the following in regard to car No. 16, of the Milwaukee Electric Railway & Light Company that has already killed four persons in this city, namely, Miss Schumacher, Eugene Sprague, Otto Segler and Lottie Tischeak. That street car companies believe in the occult and in mysterious happenings just the same as some individuals is evidenced by the action of the representatives of the Milwaukee company who have "laid up" car No. 10 because no doubt of the fact that it has proven a hoodoo to the corporation.

Within a year four persons have died as a result of coming in contact with the wheels of this modern juggernaut. The most trag-

ic of the accidents were the deaths of a young woman and a young man, not long since, who collided on bicycles and were thrown together under the car just as it was unfortunately passing. A few days ago a little girl was crushed to death by the car. Since then the company has evidently decided to sidetrack this dangerous piece of property, as it has not been continued in public use.

Patrons on the car line are also evidently afraid of the car, for its income has been much smaller than the other cars and the people who are superstitious avoid it as they would a plague. A charge of motormen has not affected the stigma which attaches to it, for the accidents have occurred under new and olf motormen. The motorman on the car when it ran over and killed two persons was so unnerved by the accident that he gave up his job and has suffered from extreme nervousness ever since. Another peculiar fact in connection with the running of street cars in Racine is that car No. 13 had been the "lucky" one of the entire system.

—*Racine Weekly Journal*
November 16, 1899

❖ ❖ ❖

Praying Woman Hit By Stray Bullet

LA CROSSE- While on her knees in prayer at the house of William DeSautelle, 1443 Avon Street, Mrs. I. F. Nuzum, wife of Reverend Nuzum of the Caledonia Street Methodist Church, was hit just above the eye with a .22-caliber bullet, which apparently had spent most of its force but had enough momentum to make a very painful wound, causing the woman's eyelid to swell up in a surprising manner.

The Ladies' Aid Society of the church was in session at the DeSautelle residence, and it is customary to begin the meetings with prayer. Mrs. Nuzum was called upon and kneeling down before a chair near a window, she began her supplications. She had only been speaking a minute when a crash has heard in the pane of the glass and Mrs. Nuzum exclaimed, "Oh, my eye is running out." This threw the woman there into confusion, but it was discovered that Mrs. Nuzum had been struck just below the eyebrow by a .22-caliber bullet, which brought blood.

The place where the bullet struck the window pane was six inches above Mrs. Nuzum's head and the only explanation given is that a spent bullet did the damage. The bullet is in the hands of the police and they are trying to locate the person who fired it. Dr. Mary Piper Houck, 1352 Caledonia Street, was called to attend Mrs. Nuzum and stated that it was not probable that the use of the injured member would be destroyed.

—*La Crosse Republican Leader*
May 12, 1900

❖ ❖ ❖

During the Civil War Wisconsin's 8th Infantry Regiment brought with them an eagle from Eau Claire. The eagle was named Old Abe in honor of President Lincoln. Old Abe was present at many battles and not one person who was in charge of holding him ever died. This fact gave Abe the reputation of having supernatural powers of protection. Abe went on to become the most famous Civil War mascot in the nation.

Bodies Are Exhumed
Road Builders At Osceola Destroy An Old Mound.
Tomb Of The Ancient Mound Builders Is Desecrated.
Bones Of The Prehistoric People Scattered Along The Turnpike.

OSCEOLA- The last vestige of the mound builders in the vicinity, which was a beautiful mound twenty-five feet in height, situated in the roadway between here and St.

Croix Falls, was demolished this week and the bones of a supposed once powerful race were strewn along the turnpike and scattered to the four winds. This mound was twenty-five feet high and forty feet in diameter at the base. It was cone-shaped and many years ago large oak trees grew on its side and summit. Being in the direct right of way for the traffic, the mound was cut away, little by little, exposing bones that had been buried for centuries, until its ruin is now complete,

One very peculiar feature about this mound was the fact that it was composed of pure black soil, while the surrounding country is either clay or sandy soil. Where this earth was secured is as mysterious as is all the work of those wonderful builders.

—*Milwaukee Journal*
November 10, 1900

❖ ❖ ❖

Sees Many Suns

WAUKESHA- August Siebner believes that he has solved the solved the secret of the solar system. He has invented an instrument which, he believes, will some day make him fabulously wealthy. Saturday afternoon Mayor Grove, Chief of Police Enders and others, at the request of Mr. Siebner, went to his home on Randal Street to see the instrument and hear his explanations of his discoveries. Before the inventor would show the gentlemen the apparatus they were obliged to swear that they would never describe it to anyone.

Mr. Siebner has had for some time the idea

that there is more than one sun. By the means of the instrument, he showed all the way from two to thirty-six suns. The numerous suns appear in a group one directly above the other. The instrument when placed in another position revels two suns some distance apart. Mr. Siebner say that he can, by means of his apparatus, bring the moon so close to earth that every line on it is discernible and he says that it is full of holes. He also tells wonderful tales of the inhabitants of the planets. He intends to take his instrument to the state observatory at Madison.

—*Milwaukee Journal*
April 22, 1901

❖ ❖ ❖

Lightning Strikes Elephant Herd
Bolt Enters A Circus Tent At Eau Claire And Kills One Of The Big Animals

EAU CLAIRE- Lightning struck the animal tent of a circus here last night killing one elephant and injuring two others. The bolt struck the menagerie tent just before eight o'clock, when about fifty men and boys were in the tent. Five elephants, two ponies and two men were knocked over. Ella, a trick elephant, got up first, and then fell dead. Parker, the trainer, says she died of fright.

There was a heavy rainstorm at the time and almost incessant lightning and thunder, and when the four other elephants revived, their trainers had difficulty in managing them. The show has been peculiarly unfortunate with elephants.

Big Charley and two other valuable beasts have been lost in the last few years. Ella was eight years old and was brought from Hagenbeck. The other elephants were greatly distressed and tried to revive her by slapping her with their trunks and one poked hay into her mouth.

—Janesville Gazette
June 29, 1901

❖ ❖ ❖

Turtle In Stomach
Eau Claire Man Complained Of Pains With Good Cause

EAU CLAIRE- A snapping turtle three inches long from the tip of the tail to the tip of the nose, was vomited by a man who came to Dr. J. H. Noble complaining of pains. He supposed the patient swallowed the turtle when it was very small.

—Milwaukee Journal
June 5, 1901

HIDDEN HEADLINES of WISCONSIN

Was Gone A Year
Baraboo Stock Buyer Disappeared And Does Not Know Where He Was

BARABOO- D.S. Holcomb, a stock breeder of this city, who disappeared a year ago, has returned. He can give no account of his wandering. A few days ago he arrived at the home of his daughter in Chicago, but could not tell where he had been. Mr. Holcomb left here for Dalton a year ago to buy stock. He did not find the man he went to see and to put in the time went fishing. As he was not seen afterwards it was thought he had drowned and search was made for the body.

Milwaukee Journal
November 7, 1901

Cut His Throat
Study of Religion Too Much For Young Man's Mind

LA CROSSE- Oscar Flickie, a boy whose parents live at DeSota, cut his throat and will probably die. For many months he has done little but speculate upon religion, and his deed is the result of the strain upon his mind.

—*Milwaukee Journal*
November 25, 1901

In 1935, due to financial struggles and a lack of jobs in the community for its students, the Morris Pratt Institute closed. In 1946 the temple was sold and a new Morris Pratt Institute building was constructed in Milwaukee where the institute continues to operate today.

Shot Firecrackers To Scare Away Goblins

LA CROSSE- A man with delirium tremens was taken into custody today. He was trying to shoot firecrackers to scare away goblins. He thought they were blockading the street car tracks.

—*Milwaukee Journal*
January 7, 1902

❖ ❖ ❖

Exploring Mounds
Possibly No Place In The State Has A Larger Mound Than Mound Cemetery

RACINE- The contents of the many mysterious mounds scattered throughout Wisconsin will doubtless before long be discovered, for the sum of $5,000 is to be raised by the archaeological section of the Natural History Society for this purpose, at Milwaukee. It was decided upon at a meeting held this week.

At this meeting attention was called to the fact that many of the best specimens of ancient pottery had been discovered in Wisconsin. Possibly there is not a spot in the great state where more mounds have and do now exist than at Mound Cemetery, the home of the dead, in the western outskirts of Racine. This burying ground is beautifully situated on elevated ground, embracing nearly fifty blocks. Sylvan Dell Creek winds its way gracefully through the grounds, and it is spanned by a handsome iron bridge. The property was purchased by Norman Clark and Mr. McKenzie, of a half-breed Indian named Wilmot, living at Buffalo, and nineteen acres of it was sold to the city in 1850.

The grounds were literally covered with mounds and a large number are still in existence, and the thousands of people who visit the grounds yearly often stand or sit on those secret places and wonder what lies beneath. No doubt this was at one time an Indian burial ground, for the reason that many Indian skeletons and instruments have been exhumed from the mounds. According to the statement made by one of the former sextons of the place, more than one hundred remains of Indians were taken up in the early days. Whether the mounds that still exist will ever be explored remains to be seen.

—Racine Daily Journal
January 18, 1902

Pyramid Near River Falls
Peculiar Geological Formation

RIVER FALLS- On the farm of Mr. Johnson, four miles north of River Falls, is one of the most peculiar pyramids to be found in the state, if not in the United States. It is a huge monument 45 feet across at the base, and 65 feet high, and looks as though it has been formed and fashioned by the hand of man. There is no other stone or rock formation in the immediate neighborhood.

The first forty feet is composed of sand stone, but the cap is of hard granite, which has protected it from the storms through all the ages, and if located in New Mexico it might easily be taken for the work of a prehistoric race.

—Milwaukee Journal
March 25, 1902

Spiritualist School
Wisconsin To Have The First Of The Kind Ever Established

WHITEWATER- The first distinctively spiritualist school ever founded is to be opened in Whitewater next September. It is to be called the Morris-Pratt Institution, and to have its quarters in a large brick building erected some years ago by Mr. Pratt, a prominent Spiritualist, at a cost of $40,000. Mr. Pratt has deeded the house to a board of trustees and promised to endow the school to the extent of $10,000, provided an equal sum be raised by the Spiritualists of Wisconsin. Psychic science will be taught in addition to the regular branches.

The board of trustees is made up of Moses Hull of Buffalo, N.Y., president; A.J. Weaver of Old Orchard, Me., superintendent; W.H. Rogers of Madison, vice-president; J.C. Bump of Milwaukee, treasurer; Mrs. Clara L. Stewart, secretary; C.L. Stevens of Pittsburg and Alonzo Thompson of Fullerton, Neb. In addition, the president of the National Spiritualist Association and the president of the Wisconsin Spiritualist Association are members of the board *ex officio.*

The annual state convention of the Wisconsin Spiritualist Association will be held in Milwaukee, April 15-17 in Lincoln Hall. Mrs. Nellie C. Moser of Kent, Oh., will act as test medium and among the speakers will be Moses Hull, W. J. Erwood of La Crosse, Mrs. McFarland of Milwaukee and Dr. Warner of Chicago. Mrs. Clara L. Stewart, president of the state association, is now here making arrangements for the convention.

—Milwaukee Journal
March 29, 1902

❖ ❖ ❖

Woman Vomits Up Live Lizard

LA CROSSE- What is believed to be a lizard was vomited up yesterday by Mrs. Mary Marshall, age 96, who makes her home with Mr. and Mrs. Lee Sieger at the Hotel Gross, 201 Vine Street. Mrs. Marshall is remembered by many old residents here as "Apple Mary" as she was once a common sight at the Cameron House depot selling apples.

Mrs. Marshall has been bothered for some time by a severe pain in her stomach and yesterday she complained more than ever, so her daughter prepared a drink for her, made mostly of Jamaica ginger and gin. This beverage must have loosened the lizard, which was evidently attached to the lining of Mary's stomach, and yesterday afternoon she vomited up the object.

She claims it was alive when it came out of her mouth but that she accidentally smothered it when she gathered it up in a handkerchief. The lizard, if it is such, is light brown in appearance and is somewhat translucent. It is the opinion of Mrs. Sieger that her mother accidentally swallowed the lizard in some water when it was very small, and that it had grown in her stomach to its present length of six inches. The animal has been places in alcohol and will be preserved.

—*La Crosse Republican Leader*
July 7, 1902

❖ ❖ ❖

Is Pronounced Dead But Life Returns

RACINE- William Johnson, aged 15 years, fell from a tree and struck square on his head, and was picked up in an unconscious condition. After working over the boy for an hour he was pronounced dead. He showed signs of life some time afterwards; restoratives were applied, and in twenty minutes the injured lad opened his eyes and asked what happened.

—*Milwaukee Journal*
July 8, 1902

❖ ❖ ❖

Young Man Writes His Own Destiny In A Song

MILWAUKEE- Thomas Kelly little thought five years ago when he wrote the song, Mother, Your Boy Will Come Home, that he was writing his own destiny, but today his song is seen to have been a prophecy. Kelly's mother, Sarah A. Kelly, died Saturday afternoon at 555 South Pierce Street at 2:42 o'clock, and several hours later the son arrived from St. Paul, Minn. Had his train been on time he would have been in time to see her alive, but she died calling for him. The strange part is that five years ago Thomas Kelly wrote a song depicting an aged mother praying her boy to come home, while he was wandering over the country. He finally decided to go, and returned only to find her cold in death. The conditions are precisely similar, through the son was at home when he wrote the song. He is a railroad man.

—*Milwaukee Journal*
August 4, 1902

on the sleeping man in spite of the rain. Drew, before he went into his long sleep announced that he would be in a hypnotic state for the rest of the week. He was attired in evening dress, and just before the lid of the coffin was set in place he made a few passes over his face and dozed off. The coffin was lowered into the grave and the grave was filled up. It is claimed that this is the first time such an experiment has been allowed to take place in this state.

—Milwaukee Journal
October 1, 1902

Mystery In Priest's Home
Pistol Shot Alarms Housekeeper, But Source Not Found

EAU CLAIRE- While Father Pappon was in his studio and his housekeeper in the kitchen, the sound of a pistol shot was heard in the kitchen and the room was filled with smoke. The housekeeper was terribly frightened, but an investigation failed to reveal any trace of a bullet and the mystery is still unexplained.

—Eau Claire Weekly Telegram
August 21, 1902

❖ ❖ ❖

Is Buried Alive
H. Drew Lowered Into Grave At Kenosha Carnival.
Says He Will Remain A Week.

KENOSHA- The opening feature of the Kenosha carnival was the burial of H. Drew, the Milwaukee baseball player, who is to remain in his grave until Saturday night. About 1,000 people surrounded the grave and later paid 10 cents to look down

❖ ❖ ❖

Hill Not Holy
Clergyman Says The Place Has Not The Miraculous Attributes Claimed

HUBERTUS- The Rev. J.J. Keenan, pastor of St. Patrick's Catholic Church in this city, declared that the so-called Holy Hill in Washington County is misnamed and that none of the marvelous and miraculous cures claimed to have been made at the shrine have stood the test of investigation. In an address on "Pilgrims and Shrines" he declared that the church had never approved Holy Hill as a shrine. He said he desired to explain the matter before the place obtained a prescriptive or antiquarian right to the claim made for it. Some years ago, he said, the papers told of a supposed marvelous cure said to have been effected for a lady of this city, but she candidly admitted a short time after that she had not benefited by her visit to the place.

—Eau Claire Weekly Telegram
August 13, 1903

CHAPTER 5 ODDITIES

His Life Is Saved By Suspender Clasp

MILWAUKEE- A steel suspender clasp saved the life of Theodore Rigas, a Plankiuton House employee, at midnight of New Year's eve. Some celebrant fired a revolver on Second St., the bullet from which, glancing, struck Rigas on the right side, puncturing overcoat, coat and vest, and denting the clasp.

—*Milwaukee Journal*
January 5, 1905

❖ ❖ ❖

He Finds Lost Watch Through Photograph

MILWAUKEE- "The Journal's Who Is He department is all right," says City Clerk Edwin Hinkel. "Years ago I missed an old silver watch which was the first I ever carried. It was given to me Dec. 2, 1880, and I hunted high and low for it, but Saturday after my picture appeared in The Journal as I was about 24 years ago. Kurtz Bros. called me up and told me that they had a watch of mine in their safe. Someone seeing my picture had thought of the old watch which contained another old picture of mine, and hunted it up to settle a bet as to whether it was Hinkel or not."

—*Milwaukee Journal*
January 23, 1905

❖ ❖ ❖

Escapes Being Buried Alive

DODGEVILLE- After arrangements had been made for her funeral, Mrs. Thomas Buckingham, who apparently died Thursday night, suddenly came to life. It is believed that she will entirely recover.

—*Marshfield Times*
July 21, 1905

Archeologists estimate that at one time Wisconsin was home to approximately 20,000 effigy mounds. However, due to development, construction, and agriculture only about 4,000 still remain.

Meet After Fifty Years, Quarrel And Part Again
Couple Who Were Engaged In Norway But Quarreled And Parted Repeat Performance

CUMBERLAND- Fifty years ago Miss Johanna Sjostrom and Andrew Swanson became engaged over in Norway. The marriage was declared off because of a quarrel. Swanson came to America. The girl married John Lynn and soon also came to the country. Swanson met the widow here by chance and a reconciliation was affected, the pair agreeing to marry. However, another quarrel occurred and they separated forever. Swanson is 80 and Mrs. Lynn 70.

—*Milwaukee Journal*
January 1, 1906

❖ ❖ ❖

La Crosse County Was Center For Mound Builders
So Says Member Of State Archeological Society.
Sun Worshippers Near Trempealeau.

TREMPEALEAU- G.H. Squier, of Trempea-leau, a member of the Wisconsin Archeological Society asserts that the center of population for the mound builders in this section if the county was at Mindoro, La Crosse County. Mr. Squier says:

The surface of the Trempealeau bluffs contain many oval mounds still. Yet I think Judge George Gale, who wrote about mounds in the county forty years ago, overestimated when he placed the Trempealeau mounds between 1,000 and 2,000. Doubtless his enumeration, which occurred in a 400-page volume, "The Upper Mississippi," included some natural elevations. The frequent appearance of platform mound near Trempealeau village is a strong evidence that a race of sun-worshippers formerly inhabited the district.

At least the peculiar locations of these mounds suggests sun-worship, and there is independent evidence that this form of

worship was practiced in some portions of the Mississippi Valley. I believe that the greatest mound builder center of population in western Wisconsin was in the Lewis Valley, near Mindoro postoffice, in the town of Farmington, La Crosse County, and stretched for perhaps half a mile eastward. Doubtless a large city was located there. For several years after the land was brought under cultivation many implements were found. Most of the mounds there were located in the finest farming land of the valley, and have been ploughed. The mounds are more abundant around Trempealeau than anywhere else in the region, but there is no corresponding abundance of implements, a perplexing condition.

The explanation may possibly be that the locality had something of a sacred character, being a place of resort for worship and perhaps for burial, rather than the permanent residence of a large number.

—*La Crosse Tribune*
August 11, 1905

❖ ❖ ❖

Police Seek Bearded Lady For Theft

LA CROSSE- "She is a heavy woman with blue eyes, light hair, and a beard like a man, and shaves three times a week." This was the apt description given by Ethal Wagner to Judge Brindley this morning of a girl whom the complainant alleged stole $36 from her while employed as a servant. The girl had worked in the Wagner home, 313 N. 2nd Street for some time and knew where Miss Wagner kept her money, according to Miss Wagner. The servant girl recently resigned her position and left for Winona, Minnesota.

A short time after her departure Miss Wagner discovered $36 was missing from her dresser where she always kept her money. She at once fixed the guilt on her ex-servant, Maud Hillyer, or Maud Conyer, as she is sometimes known. A warrant for the girl's arrest was taken out this morning and Sheriff Lins of Winona will endeavor to locate the girl.

—*La Crosse Tribune*
September 12, 1905

❖ ❖ ❖

Very Peculiar
Snake Story
Comes From North Side Hill.
Cow Said To Have
Snake In Stomach.

EAU CLAIRE- A most peculiar snake story comes from the north side to the effect that a cow owned by a widow lady on Madison Street took sick and continued to get worse until it became necessary to kill the beast, which was done. Satisfied that there was some internal trouble an examination was made and it is said a snake, closely resembling a water snake in appearance, about an inch and a half thick and nearly fifteen feet long was found in the stomach of the cow. It is said that neighbors are willing to corroborate this statement.

—*Eau Claire Leader*
March 2, 190

Religious Books
Cause Insanity
A Superior Boy Conversed With
Angels From Reading Literature

SUPERIOR- Constant reading of religious books is said to have caused Alex Sherburn to become insane and taken to Mendota asylum. He had many times asked friends to converse with angels. The young man has no relatives in this country.

—*Eau Claire Leader*
November 29, 1905

❖ ❖ ❖

A False Report

IOLA- James Mulligan of Iola Wis., narrowly escaped being buried alive

Thursday. The funeral procession was slowly wending its way to the church when the driver of the hearse heard groans from within, following by smashing of glass. The casket was opened and Mulligan, fully restored to consciousness, sat up and began to inquire where he was.

He had been in a trance for three days. The above appeared in the city paper last week dated from Loyal. The post master at Iowa has since published a statement to the effect that no such occurrence has been heard of in his town.

—*Marshfield Times*
March 2, 1906

❖❖❖

Cursed City Still There
Preacher's Prophecy Fails And Scared Madison Folk Return

MADISON- Sheepishly, quiet and shame-facedly, 1,500 residents of Madison came back to their homes last night after having spent twenty-fours hours in waiting to hear that Madison had sunk and been engulfed by the inrush of the waters of the surrounding lakes. The prophecy of religious exhorter, which created consternation among certain residents, did not come true. He declared that the lakes would rise up and engulf the city. The man who made the prediction called himself "Professor Jones." He held religious meetings on the streets and was arrested for obstructing traffic. Then he cursed the city and made his prediction. Newspapers took up the matter and hundreds of persons last night

left the city. There was no disturbance here today. The people went to summer parks, baseball games and other amusement places as usual.

—*Eau Claire Leader*
June 19, 1906

❖❖❖

Heartbroken Dog Commits Suicide

LA CROSSE- Humiliated and heartbroken, a little black dog belonging to Hutchinson & Manning of the north side deliberately committed suicide yesterday by laying on the streetcar tracks in front of the store and allowing a car to run over him.

During the afternoon the dog was ordered out of the Hutchinson's Saloon, 620 Copeland Avenue, and given a kick on his way out. Not used to this kind of treatment, the animal seemed to take the humiliation to heart and drooping his head, he sulked into the street and deliberately laid down his head on a streetcar rail.

When the streetcar approached the dog, the motorman clanged the bell loudly but the dog refused to move. Witnesses say the little canine looked out of the corners of his eyes at the approaching car and then closed his eyes and waited for the end. His head was completely severed from his body by the wheels of the streetcar. Those who witnessed the peculiar incident declare it was a case of suicide, pure and simply.

—*La Crosse Tribune*
July 17, 1906

CHAPTER 5 ODDITIES

Finds Skeleton Of Giant
Well Preserved Implements Are Dug Up In The City Of Trempealeau

TREMPEALEAU- Excavators removing soil for a new sidewalk a half block south of Main Street uncovered the bones of what is believed to have been a mound builder, also some well-preserved stone implements, weapons, pottery and an oven, presumably of prehistoric origin. Earnest Bright made the discovery. He saw part of a skull protruding from the damp earth and after digging a few feet below the surface the spinal column and other bones were found. Trempealeau citizens say the bones are either those of an Indian of unusual size or of a mound builder, which archaeological researchers have proved lived in the vicinity of Trempealeau. The latter theory is more generally accepted, because of the array of stone implements found with the bones. A clay oven was found imbedded in the dirt. Many dishes of a brackish cast and made of a peculiar stone were also found.

—*Eau Claire Leader*
July 19, 1906

❖ ❖ ❖

Claims Hoodoo Clings To Family

DRYWOOD- The children of Bert Tandler, who murdered his wife at Milton Junction and then committed suicide at Eau Claire, Sept 8, have been adopted by Mr. and Mrs. White, who reside at Drywood, Chippewa County. At the hearing it was learned that the Tandler family seems to have been born under an unlucky star. The elder Tandler came from Germany and settled at Drywood. Illness has visited various members of the family; then they have had misfortune almost every year. In July, the home of the family was burned down and much money and many valuable papers were lost. Members of the family were afraid to adopt the children.

—*Eau Claire Leader*
October 11, 1906

❖ ❖ ❖

Digs Up Skeleton Near Lake Ripley

LAKE RIPLEY- The eleventh skeleton that has been dug up in this neighborhood in the last five years was discovered by A.E. Morton while he was excavating for his home on Lake Ripley. The skeleton was entire, and is supposed to be that of an Indian. An unusual feature is the double set of teeth in the lower jaw. The skeleton measured six feet three inches from head to base of foot. It will no doubt be presented to the state historical museum at Madison by Mr. Morton.

—*Eau Claire Leader*
November 27, 1907

❖ ❖ ❖

Mystery Baffles La Crosse People

LA CROSSE- A great mystery is puzzling the people of La Crosse. It is wailed

around by the mystic name "The Demateos." A thousand people a day are trying to unravel it. The Demateos are the sensation at the Unique Theatre this week. Their wonderful jests whether of legendary main or black art, whether the product of occult powers or inimitable trickery, are the most remarkable character.

Demateo is one of the niftiest performers in the line of handcuff manipulation, etc., in the business, but the great feature of his act is that in which he places his wife in a mail sack, has it securely locked and examined by members of the audience and gets her out of the bag within forty seconds without unlocking it. Crowds are studying the performance and attempting to solve the mystery. At two performances this week Manager Michinsky will give away a gold watch to patrons of the house.

—*La Crosse Tribune*
October 29, 1906

❖ ❖ ❖

The Great Stone Face
Wonderful Likeness
Discovered By Engineers.
Seems Almost Human.
Found In A Secluded Nook Of The
Old River Bed.

KILBOURN- Kilbourn seems to be the center of the wonderful workings of nature and in every direction may be found curiously formed pieces of rock which have been cut away by the erosive action of the water, and left to be admired and pondered at by the thousands of tourists who visit the Dells during the tourist season, from the first of June until the latter part of October.

Within a very short distance of the city may be found curiously shaped mounds resembling different animals in form and in many instances hundreds of feet in length. There are pieces, however, that are exceedingly wonderful, that are very seldom visited by our summer tourists, and among these and perhaps the most wonderful of all is the Old River Bed as it is usually called. This was the original channel of the river, hundreds of years ago, and starts across from the Larks Hotel in the Dells and runs for several miles west of the river and finally swings south and back to the channel.

There are a great many of the channels which were formed at different periods, but the one above mentioned is by far the most curious on account of the wonderful rock formations. The rocks in many places rise in a perpendicular precipice for a hundred feet or more above the marshy bottom. It is almost impossible for a person to transverse this channel except in the winter when the ground is frozen as the entire course in an oozy marsh. A lover of nature is doubly repaid for a long and difficult jaunt, however, by the wonderful formations, sometimes in the form of a rocky island jutting up out of the channel and in other places a huge crevice or cave extending back a great many feet into the rock walls.

For some time back the civic engineers, under V.H. Reineking, who are doing field work for the Southern Wisconsin Power Co., which is putting in the 10,000 horse power water plant at Kilbourn, have been gathering data for their work and this takes them into every ravine and nearly every crevice of rock within a radius of several miles of the proposed dam. While out on research work recently in the Old River Bed, the party was running a line up a side ravine and by accident came upon a perfect face of stone on a solid rock cliff. Later a photograph was taken and a reproduction made for the Mirror-Gazette.

Its origin is a mystery and there is no way of telling when or how the face was formed, although it is very evident that it is the work of a human hand. The face is in a sheltered nook but the rock is discolored and moss grows with age. It is with great difficulty that the stone face can be reached and being located in this out-of-the-way place it is probable that the people of this section up to the present have been ignorant of its existence.

—The Kilbourn Gazette
March 7, 1907

Kilbourn City was established in 1857 where railroad tracks crossed the Wisconsin River. In 1931, the name of the city was changed from Kilbourn to its present name of Wisconsin Dells.

Superior Claims Rockefeller
Believed That Oil King's Father Lived At Head Of Lakes

SUPERIOR- Since the report that John D. Rockefeller's father lived for a time in "a city by the lake" in Wisconsin and was buried at Blair, Trempealeau County, local residents recall the mysterious W.A. Bradley, or Gardner as he was also known, who appeared here in 1900 and opened up a patent medicine business which earned him the title of "Dr."

HIDDEN HEADLINES of WISCONSIN

Occasionally, when with convivial companions, he would declare that if he were to demand his rights from his people, he would not only not have to work, but he would be a conspicuous figure in the eyes of the world. He made no secret of the fact that he was living under an assumed name. Bradley or Gardner, left Superior in 1904 and in 1906 it was reported that he died and was buried at Blair.

—*Milwaukee Journal*
January 9, 1908

Rockefeller's father, William Avery Rockefeller, passed away on May 11, 1906. His place of death was "officially" listed as Freeport, Illinois, where he was said to be buried in Oakland Cemetery.

Milwaukee Earthquake
A Few Further Particulars Taken From Our Exchanges

MILWAUKEE- The shock was sufficiently strong to cause pictures or walls to sway in an uncanny manner. Workers at desks felt their swivel chairs rock and in private homes, dishes rattled ominously in the pantry shelves. The shock at 8:40 o'clock was felt by hundreds of Milwaukee people and by residents in Wauwatosa and other places in the county. Some of the largest business buildings in the city received the shock, according to various occupants, and at the Colby & Abbot building, corner of Milwaukee and Mason Streets, many of the tenants were almost panic stricken for a moment. The shock was so decided that in several offices the water bottles resting on small shelves against the walls were knocked to the floor. E.C. Wall, former president of the chamber of commerce, was shaken in his chair at his residence on Knapp Street, where he was sitting at a desk writing.

At Madison a slight earthquake was experienced at 8:38 on May 26. The shock was noted at the local weather bureau and by the Washburn observatory at the university, but there are no instruments in the city for recording shocks. Prof. William H. Hobbs, an expert on earthquakes and a former instructor at the university and now with the University of Michigan, who is a guest of President and Mrs. Van Hise, declared this morning he noticed three distinct shocks.

Reports from nearby cities indicate that the tremor was felt more distinctly inland than in this immediate vicinity. At the office of the weather bureau, where the moods of nature are made a matter of study, there are no instruments for recording the vibrations of the earth, but it was observed that framed pictures on the walls swayed quite perceptibly. "I was conscious of a slight but distinctly noticeable trembling of the building," said Maj. Hersey, who was in his office on the fourth floor of the federal building at the time. "It was a motion such as might have been felt in a slight framed building when a strong wind is blowing, but under the circumstances I was convinced at once that it was an earthquake. For fifteen seconds the movements continued, its violence neither increasing nor diminishing during his time. Then it ceased suddenly. We have no instruments which record seismic disturbances and I have no means of getting accurate information, concerning the shock."

The tremor was felt throughout the federal building. Assistant Custodian E.D. Moe closed the glass cover of a cabinet which swayed to and fro with the motion of the building. The effect was less apparent on the lower floors of the building. Attorney William C. Quarles was dictating to a stenographer in his office on the fifth floor of the Sentinel building. He felt the quake when it began, but did not realize what it was until more than half of it was over. In the courthouse the shock was felt slightly. Elkhorn also felt the shock. It lasted several seconds, was felt through the city and county at 8:37 o'clock. At places, dishes were knocked from shelves and clocks stopped by the shock.

—*Eau Claire Leader*
May 28, 1909

❖ ❖ ❖

Kidnap Attempt Made On Carnival Dwarf

LA CROSSE- A deliberate attempt to kidnap Nicholi, the little Russian prince who is being exhibited with the Kline Shows at the northside carnival, occurred last evening about closing time of the show.

The Prince is only 25 inches tall and weighs 16 pounds. Mrs. Blitz, wife of the manager of the Russian prince, was startled to hear cries from the midget, whom she had left standing on the platform alone while she went to get a little fresh air after an arduous evening's performance at the carnival. When she rushed to the front the Prince was gone and a stranger was seen dashing away. He had not gone far, and as she could see nothing of the Prince, Mrs. Blitz supposed that he was hidden somewhere under the man's top coat.

Her theory later proved to be correct, for the Prince himself says that he was nearly smothered in an outside pouch or pocket of the man's coat. The Prince's weak little voice could scarcely be heard as he cried for help, and probably for that reason those who saw the man hastening away thought nothing of what was going on. Mrs. Blitz called to her husband and together they hurried to the entrance of the carnival lot and headed off the man.

When they reached him he was in the act of springing into an auto. Mrs. Blitz caught hold of him and held him fast while her husband extracted the Prince from a bulging, pouch-like pocket inside the man's coat. The stranger broke Mrs. Blitz's hold and jumped into the auto and soon disappeared from sight. A similar attempt was made to steal the Prince when he was being exhibited in the west a few weeks ago, but that scheme dis not come so near being successful as last night's incident. Mrs. Blitz's thinks a party of rival showmen want to kidnap the two-foot man for their own profit.

Prince Nicholi, when seen last night following the kidnap attempt said, "My, oh my, but that was a close shave. I was awful scared when I was plunked down in the man's pocket. It seemed like being put into a bag. He put me in head first and I nearly smothered before I was able to wiggle around and get on my feet. Even then it was uncomfortable, for the fellow who had me was running and I kept bumping against his legs. But Daddy Blitz was Johnny at the rat hole and here I am."

The northside carnival was set up mainly on the street in the 700 and 800 block of Rose Street with nearby Hagar, St. Cloud, and St. James Streets also occupied.

—*La Crosse Tribune*
June 9, 1909

❖ ❖ ❖

Thought End Of World Had Come

HARTLAND- A strange light in the northern skies, taking the shape of a comet, then various fanciful outlines the other evening made the superstitious people of this village believe the end of the world was at hand. Several families spent the night in chairs with wraps on, in fear of the phenomenon. In the morning it was discovered that the cause was a fire in Hustisford.

—*La Crosse Tribune*
March 19, 1908

❖ ❖ ❖

Old Clock Stops When Owner Dies

MANITOWOC- Charles T. Dobbert, pioneer tanner and one of the oldest residents of this city, died at the age of 78 years last night from the infirmities of old age. Mr. Dobbert died at 4:25, and just at that hour the family clock, which had been in the Dobbert family for forty years, ceased its labors. Mr. Dobbert came here more in his youth as a shoemaker and established a tannin plant which he continued for more than forty years. He had served as a member of the council, has been on the school board and was prominent as a businessman in earlier days. A family of five children, all except one residents of this city, survives. The funeral will be on Wednesday.

—*Eau Claire Leader*
July 21, 1909

❖ ❖ ❖

Meteorite Found On Puffer Farm
Fell Thirty Years Ago And No Trace Of It Could Be Found Until Now. Composed Of Solid Stone. Cause Of meteors Is Admitted To Be Something That Enters The Earth's Atmosphere From Without. Average Velocity Of Meteors Is Thirty Miles A Second.

MOUNT PLEASANT- George Puffer brought to the Journal office yesterday a perfect meteorite which fell from the heavens thirty years ago, on the E.C. Puffer farm in the town of Mt. Pleasant. At the time it dropped, Mr. E.C. Puffer, now deceased, occupied the farm and hundreds of farmers witnessed the falling of the stone accompanied by a trial of light and illumination. Some of the farmers searched for the meteorite, but failed to find it. A short time ago George Puffer and others were walking around the farm and found the long-looked for meteorite and it is now on exhibition at this office. It weighs about a pound, is solid stone, and in many respects resembles a small cannon ball.

According to history, a number of meteorites have fallen in Wisconsin during the past forty years, at least three in Racine County. The most remarkable of all meteors are those which are followed by the falling of stones in the earth. These have since the beginning of the present century attracted so much attention, and the phenomena have been so frequently examined and described by scientific men, that they are very well understood. The circumstances accompanying the fall of stone are tolerably uniform. A ball of fire crosses the sky so bright as to be visible if it appears in the daytime, sometimes even at hundreds of miles from the meteor, and if it appears in the night it is bright enough to light up the whole landscape.

It traverses the sky, generally finishing its course in a few seconds. It suddenly goes out even with or without an apparent bursting into pieces and after a short period a loud detonation in all of the region near the place where the meteor has disappeared. Sometimes only a single stone and sometimes several are found. For some falls they are numbered by the thousands. These meteorites leave behind them in the air a cloud or train that may disappear in a few seconds or remain for an hour. They come at all times of the day, and all seasons of the year, and in all regions of the earth. They come irrespective of the phases of the weather except as clouds conceal them from view.

At one time in Nebraska, the falling of meteors was followed by such loud explosions that the people were frightened, even the animals in the fields being alarmed. At one time in Indiana, a farmer heard a heavy thud of an object striking the ground over his house. The next morning he found on the snow a stone of very peculiar appearance weighing three-quarters of a pound, which from its appearance came from a meteor. This stone from a published description, was in many respects the same as found on the Puffer farm, and described above. In many of the museums of the country can be found stones of various sizes and appearance which came from meteors.

The average velocity of meteors is thirty miles a second. The cause of meteors is universally admitted to be something that enters the earth's atmosphere from without with a velocity relative to the earth that is comparable to the earth's velocity in its orbit, which is 19 miles per second. By the resistance it meets in penetrating the air the light and phenomena of the luminous train are produced. Under favorable circumstances portions of these bodies reach the earth's surface as meteorites.

—*Racine Daily Journal*
September 28, 1909

Eight Foot
Skeleton Found

FERRYVILLE- The skeleton of a pre-historic man, which assembled, indicated that the being whose bones were found by C.H. Lawrence of Ferryville, measured eight or nine feet in height, has been unearthed near Viroqua and is attracting great curiosity and attention.

Together with the skeleton are many other bones of the same nature and larger than the normal size. Three complete jaw bones have been found among the collection, in each of which all of the teeth are intact and perfect, although in one of the specimen the molars have been shortened by wear to the level of the gums.

A peculiarity of the teeth is that the molars are wore more on the left side than on the right indicating that the beings in life chewed and knawed principally on that side. The skeleton and bones were unearthed in the mound as it is thought that the bones are from the mound building age, of men who have lived centuries before the white man discovered America.

—Cashton Record
October 1, 1909

Farmers Take Lightning
Rods From Buildings

NEENAH- Fearful that the rods might attract dangerous substances that might accompany the comet today, many farmers in this vicinity removed the lightning rods from their homes and barns and took other precautions. In the Polish settlement of this city the families will remain in their homes in prayer.

—Racine Daily Journal
May 18, 1910

❖ ❖ ❖

An Earthquake At
Milwaukee
Marquette University Seismograph
Locates An Earthquake Somewhere
But Doesn't Know Where

MILWAUKEE- A violent unlocated earthquake was recorded at Washington and elsewhere this morning by the Marquette University seismograph. Preliminary tremors began at 5:05 and were especially noticeable in the north and south needle. At 5:11 the east needle started an oscillation followed by two other maximums at 5:15 and 5:18. The shock seemed to come from the south or southwest.

—Eau Claire Leader
January 2, 1910

The average height for an American male in 1909 was 5 feet 6 inches.

Wants Prayer To God For Rain
Some Unknown Person Sends Written Request For Publication. Asks Ministers And Priests To Have Bells Tolled At That Time.

EAU CLAIRE- The following unique request, written with pencil and by an unknown person, came to the Leader office and although it was received too late for Sunday's paper, it is given now. We have had no rain since Sunday. So that the request is not too late please put in large print and place to be easily seen, in Sunday's paper only –July 2, 1910: "Will the brothers and sisters in Christ, all unite in prayer, either in their homes or in the churches tomorrow, at 2 o'clock to God, to send us rain and let the ministers and priests see that the bells are tolled in the churches at that hour. IN JESUS' NAME, WE ASK IT." "P.S. Please send a copy to all the ministers and priests in Eau Claire." The above was not signed. It is not too late to take action. For the past week or more, prayers have been offered in the majority of the churches asking for rain. At Nearly every service, prayers with this request were offered.

—*Eau Claire Leader*
July 5, 1910

Problem Unsolved But Man Is Crazy
Manitowoc Carpenter Goes Insane Working Over Problem Of The Fourth Dimension

MANITOWOC- Algebra and the fourth dimension problem is said to be responsible for the insanity of Theodore Sprecht, a carpenter who, since a recent debate on the fourth dimension, has spent his time trying to solve the problem.

—*Janesville Daily Gazette*
August 17, 1910

Wikipedia lists the fourth dimension as: "The concept of a fourth dimension is one that is often described in considering its physical implications, that is, we know that in three dimensions, we have dimensions of length, width, and height. The fourth dimension is said to be at right angles to these three, and is often described as time."

> The American Heritage Dictionary defines the Fourth Dimension as: "Time regarded as a coordinate dimension and required by relativity theory, along with three spatial dimensions, to specify completely the location of any event."

Unique Find In Digging A Well
Strange Specimens Brought To The Surface In Shawtown Brings To Mind Paragraphs From Historical Pages

SHAWTOWN- Can it be that once upon a time giant animals and human persons roamed about in the vicinity of Shawtown, only some two hundred feet lower down? And can it be that all of a sudden a land slide rushed down and buried everything? Anyhow, something strange has come to pass in the digging of a well below Shawtown and which has caused many to look in the pages of history.

It is this way—Chas. Jones, 1637 Menomonie Street, who is foreman for Mrs. Oliver Sweet, owner of a well-digging apparatus, has been sinking a well on the place of Chas. Fleming in the Town of Union and which comes up to Shawtown. When down 158 feet we thought there were queer things in sight. He hauled up everything and to his surprise found clogged in the sand-bucket chunks of wood, pieces of limbs of trees and a mineral resembling silver growing onto one of the limbs.

Now the question arises as to how such things could be so far below the surface and when all traces of anyone sinking a well there before have proven futile. Many examining the specimens, some well-versed in historical specimens, say they must belong to a period before the flood. No doubt, they say strange animals roamed the face of the earth in those days, millions of years ago, and browsed on these trees. Many of the specimens appeared to be petrified and the wood much resembling the cedar.

—*Eau Claire Daily Leader*
September 2, 1910

> The first practical typewriter was designed in Milwaukee during 1867.

Queer Spontaneous Combustion

MILWAUKEE- Shortly after 9 o'clock yesterday morning, the firemen were called to No. 859, Third Street, by an alarm from Box 476. The building, which is a two-story brick, is occupied by John Roehring, Supervisor from the Thirteenth Ward. One of the family who was abed had found the room filling with smoke, and jumped from the window to a shed, giving alarm. When the firemen got to the scene of the commotion they were considerably nonplussed. The chimney which was thought to be at fault was all right. Finally the door to a closet off the bedroom was opened and inside was found to be the blaze.

The plastering was broken through and the flames squelched, the loss being only about $30. It was a narrow escape, though. No reason, whatever, can be given for the lively blaze. There was nothing in the closet but shoes and clothes, and no chimney flue ran anywhere near it. There was no oil stored anywhere, either. It is a singular case, and the Chief considers it an instance of pure, unadulterated spontaneous combustion—minus the usual rags and oil.

—*Milwaukee Daily Sentinel*
February 2, 1880

Wild Man

VERONA- In the yard was a wild man chained to a log. He lived in the woods here, and was the terror of the neighborhood many years ago, we learn. Nothing is known, we believe, respecting his history.

—Wisconsin State Journal
May 21, 1870

❖ ❖ ❖

Strange Behavior

EMBARRASS- A man named Peter Urquhard, of Embarrass, has been cutting up queer antics, his mind, which has lately been somewhat unsettled, gave way entire-ly and he was possessed with the notion that he ought to offer a sacrifice of his cow, his pigs and one of his children. He killed the cow with the pitchfork, his pigs with a spade, and was endeavoring to kill his boy, when the screams of his wife brought help, and he was carried off. However, while his captors were not looking, he escaped and ran back two miles to his house, and again tried to kill his child, but his pursuers were too close at his heels, and he was again taken into custody and safely lodged in jail. He was a hard-working citizen and universally respected.

—Waupaca Republican
April 30, 1881

❖ ❖ ❖

Death Breaks Very Long Fast
The Rev. A.D. Hendrickson Of Janesville Expires At Last.
Had Eaten No Food For Forty-Seven And A Half Days.
One Of The Most Remarkable Cases Of Which There Is Any Record.

JANESVILLE- After a fast covering forty-seven and a half days, the Rev. A. D. Hendrickson, a retired Methodist divine, passed away at 9:45 o'clock this morning. He was 75 years of age, and took to his bed in December, as the result of a stroke of paralysis. Nothing but water had passed his lips since Dec. 1 and he passed away as if in sleep.

For three or four days after he was stricken. Mr. Hendrickson was unable to move a muscle on the left side. Then he gradually recovered the use of most of his muscles. Food, however, seemed to be repugnant to him, its sight irritating him exceedingly. A second stroke Dec. 10 seemed to affect his head and after that he was unable to swallow anything except water.

Mr. Hendrickson has been well-known in Wisconsin for more than forty years. He was superintendent of the reform school at Waukesha from 1865 to 1877, previous to which he served two years as county superintendent of schools. He came to Wisconsin from New York in 1855 and engaged in teaching school at Eagle, Waukesha County, where he remained several years. In 1872 he was sent by the state to the International Penal Association at London.

—Milwaukee Journal
January 17, 1899

❖❖❖

Wore Only A Wrapper
Mrs. Leonard Walks Eleven Miles And Carries Her Babe

CRIVITZ- Sheriff Nelson took Mrs. Amelia Leonard, the wife of a farmer at Crivitz, to the Oshkosh asylum, where she was formerly an inmate, but had been discharged as cured. Monday night the woman left her husband, who was ill of typhoid fever, and dressed in a calico wrapper, walked eleven miles with her baby in her arms. She was found this morning in a demented condition and was again sent to the asylum.

—Milwaukee Journal
January 17, 1900

Boy Would Hunt Indians
Ray Marsden Of Fond du Lac Has Disappeared

FOND DU LAC- Ray Marsday, a 13-old-boy who was educated principally from dime novels, armed himself with a revolver and a knife and started out to hunt Indians. At Milwaukee he was arrested and disarmed, the police releasing him on the promise that he would return home. He has not reached here, however, and his wanderings. This is the same boy who left Oct. 24, last, and for two weeks wandered about the pineries in the north where he was finally located.

—Milwaukee Journal
April 13, 1900

An Insane Man Burns A Lumber Camp

MARINETTE- Chauncey Raymond, a lumberjack who was watching camp on Sturgeon River became suddenly insane yesterday and set fire to the camp and the entire outfit, causing a loss of several thousand dollars. He then fled through the woods with an ax and attacked a driving crew camped near Vulcan, Mich. He almost killed one man and the entire crew fled with the insane man in chase. He was finally subdued and tied down.

—Milwaukee Journal
May 4, 1900

❖ ❖ ❖

Wild Man In The Woods

GRANTSBURG- A wild man is terrorizing the people north of here. He appears to be about 35 years of age, has long black whiskers, is barefooted, has scarcely any clothing on him and he carries a hatchet. He secrets himself in the woods during the day and gives the most bloodcurdling yells. The sheriff has been unable to capture the man.

—Milwaukee Journal
June 25, 1900

❖ ❖ ❖

Snake Eater
Visits La Crosse

LA CROSSE- There is a woman at a hotel on Pearl Street who eats snakes. She is closely guarded in a room on the third floor, where she wiles away the weary hours devouring the heads of rattlesnakes. Her name is Bosco and in many ways she resembles a snake. Her owner is a Klondiker who went broke and says that she is the best claim he ever struck.

Bosco is awful to look at. Two repulsive tusks (eyeteeth) protrude from her mouth, and when she buries those weapons into the neck of her victim, it's not long before the head of the snake drops down her throat while its body coils on the ground to become lifeless when the sun goes down. Bosco is unable to walk. She is carried about in an invalid's chair that has a canvas spread over it to hide her from the morbid curiosity of the public. She is perfectly harmless unless her teeth come in contact with some fleshy substance. She then becomes the snake eater and devourer of anything that contains blood.

Yesterday she was brought to La Crosse and her owner tried to get a license of exhibit from the city for his "find." The ordinance providing for exhibitions of this nature requires a license fee of $125, which made the manager decide he would not spend any time in this city. "Bosco eats snakes," he said, "and crowds would have given two bits to see her devour them, but I can't afford to pay $125 for the privilege of exhibiting her for a day and a night."

"Bosco has a history," her manager continued. "She was an Abyssinian and when born she was deformed and according to Abyssinian religious beliefs, all deformed babies must be given to the snakes. She met that fate, but the bite of the reptile did not prove fatal and she at once became a curiosity. She lived with those horrible creatures and finally began to eat them," he said. "Her system is immuned with poison and the only effect a snake bite has upon her is that it causes a sleepy sensations to come over her. Her skin is copper color and she is worth her weight in gold," he added.

The clerks and chambermaids at her Pearl Street hotel perform their daily duties with trepidation. The female employees refuse to frequent the third floor where her room is and would rather starve than get within two floors of the snake-like woman. Both the day and night staff have kept their eyes wide open while on duty for fear that Bosco will sneak upon them and take a nibble at their heads. At the Winona, Minn. street fair it is said Bosco buried her teeth in the clothes of a curious boy, nearly disrobing the frightened lad.

—*La Crosse Daily Press*
September 17, 1900

❖ ❖ ❖

Madison Girl Wears Shoes Made From Human Skin

MADISON- Miss Myrtle E. Downing is wearing a pair of low shoes made from human skin sent to her by a Madison boy who is attending a medical college in Chicago. The shoes are a light tan color, with black toes and black stitching. They are very pretty and Miss Downing is very proud of them. She paraded the street this morning, accompanied by two girl friends, and exhibited the shoes to a great many curious people. These shoes possess additional interest to Miss Downing from the fact that the skin from which they are made was taken from the leg of an unknown man who was murdered in the streets of Chicago.

Mrs. Downing, in speaking of the matter, showed considerable pride in her daughter's shoes and said she knew of no reason why she should not wear them. "Myrtle is a member of the Presbyterian church," said she, "One of the church members said to her, 'I do not see that there is any sin in it.'" Mrs. Downing explained the manner in which students worked in the dissecting rooms. "You know," she said, "the first thing they do is to peel the body." She said that Myrtle had a picture sent to her where the boys were peeling bodies.

Myrtle is a pretty girl, 18 years of age, and was graduated from the high school last June. Her father, Joseph Downing, is a traveling man. Miss Downing received more than enough tanned human hide to make the pair of shoes. She is "thinking up" something else to make out of the remainder, perhaps a pocket book.

—*Milwaukee Journal*
October 10, 1900

❖ ❖ ❖

Gone To Hunt Indians

MILWAUKEE- John Milentz, a 9-year-old boy is missing from his home at 317 State Street and his mother fears that he has started on an expedition to kill Indians. He had been talking about going with an older boy whom the mother does not know, and when he was taken to school by his mother Friday morning he objected. While she was talking to the principal he slipped away and has not been home since. It is supposed that the boys started out into the country and will soon be found.

—*Milwaukee Journal*
October 1, 1900

Boy Acts Like Mad Dog

LA CROSSE- Sheriff Barber was called upon late Saturday night to take charge of a 17-year-old boy named Phillip Linn, who was creating a great disturbance in the neighborhood of 13th and La Crosse Streets by his peculiar actions, similar to those of a mad dog. When the Sheriff arrived at the scene Linn was being held on the sidewalk by six strong husky men and he was snapping and biting at everything he saw or could reach.

He was taken to the county jail where today he was examined by Drs. John Rowles and George E. Powell, who found that he was sane and suffering from cerebral congestion with all the symptoms of meningitis. The boy was then taken to La Crosse Hospital, 1306 Badger Street, where he is now resting easy. It is said that the boy was kicked in the head by a horse a couple of years ago and was also sunstruck last year, which no doubt are responsible for his present pitiable condition.

—*La Crosse Republican Leader*
July 1, 1901

In 1900, the average life expectancy was 47 years.

CHAPTER 6 PECULIAR PEOPLE

Racine Man Snarls Like Dog

RACINE- A man 21 years old, living in this city, lies at his home in a precarious condition as a result of having been bitten by a dog eleven years ago. The young man is said to bite and snarl like a dog and at times it takes the combined efforts of four men to hold him.

—Milwaukee Journal
October 26, 1901

❖❖❖

Insanity From Insomnia
Peshtigo Man's Mind Shattered From Loss Of Sleep

MARINETTE- Carl Schmidt, a well-known Peshtigo man, was brought here for examination as to his sanity. He has not slept for a month and is now wholly irresponsible.

—Milwaukee Journal
March 8, 1902

❖❖❖

Insane From Lightning
Peculiar Malady Affects Kenosha Man During Storms

KENOSHA- A peculiar malady which is proving an enigma to the physicians is affecting John Gunniston. Several times during the last month Gunniston has become violently insane, during the prevalence of electric storms, but as soon as the storm has passed the reason of the man had returned and he has been just the same as ever. Gunniston seems to be well acquainted with his malady and with the approach of the storms he has repeatedly asked members of his family to lock him in his room. He was struck by lighting three years ago.

—Milwaukee Journal
July 19, 1902

❖❖❖

Young Man Is Insane From Cigarettes

CUMBERLAND- George Holmberg, son of the Methodist minister at this place, went insane yesterday from smoking cigarettes.

—Milwaukee Journal
January 10, 1903

❖❖❖

Insane From Cigarettes
Face And Hands Of Juneau Man Turn Yellow

JUNEAU- A young man giving his name as C.G. McAllister, whose deranged mental state it is said is caused from the excessive use of cigarettes, has been taken to the insane asylum. The skin of his hands and face have assumed a yellowish color. He came here as a tramp and was poorly dressed.

—Milwaukee Journal
April 21, 1902

HIDDEN HEADLINES of WISCONSIN

Strange Maniac Eats Hay
Beats Boulders With Fence Rail Until Exhausted And Captured

GERMANTOWN- A raving lunatic having all the appearance of a real wild man terrorized some of the farmers in the southeastern part of Germantown. When first seen he amused himself by rolling large boulders into the roadway and with a fence rail beat these until he became exhausted. A number of farmers brought him to Rockford and notified Sheriff Hilt, and his deputy, Fred Schloemer, took him to the Northern Hospital. Among a bundle of clothes which he carried was a slip of paper upon which was written Henry Sastric, Chicago.

> —*Eau Claire Weekly Telegram*
> August 20, 1903

❖ ❖ ❖

Is A Human Monster
Child Is Half Dog And Half Man

MARINETTE- A human monstrosity, half dog and half man, was born here. The child is living and the mother seems as fond of it as though normal, and insists on keeping it alive, regardless of medical advice that it be allowed to die. The body is covered with hair and has a long, projecting nose and a low forehead. It is said that the mother was scared by a dog jumping on her about a month ago.

> —*Eau Claire Leader*
> February 3, 1905

❖ ❖ ❖

Laura Ingalls Wilder was born in Pepin in 1867.

Girl Terrifies Neighbors By Howling Like Dog

LA CROSSE- Howling day and night like a dog in distress, Hilda Johnson, a feebleminded girl residing at 1448 Caledonia Street, is terrifying residents of the vicinity, and a number of vacant houses in that neighborhood attest to the fact.

The case, which has recently been called to the attention of the authorities, is a pitiful one. The girl, who is 17 years old, has been feebleminded since birth and has had to be constantly watched and kept within bounds for fear that something serious might happen. Of late, her dementia has taken an unusually severe form in the nature of long, hideous howls, like those of a dog, which startle passersby and keep people in the vicinity awake at night.

Several families have moved out of the neighborhood as a result of the girl's hideous noises. One family there sold their home, in which they had lived for years, and purchased a residence in another section of the city because of this cause. The girl should not be taken to the state asylum at Mendota, the authorities say, but rather should be placed at the Home for Feebleminded at Chippewa Falls. However, an effort to place her in that institution failed, and local authorities are now in a dilemma. The case will be taken up with the Board of Control and another effort will be made to have the girl admitted to the institution at Chippewa Falls.

—*La Crosse Tribune*
July 20, 1905

❖ ❖ ❖

Man Goes 60 Years Without Bath

LA CROSSE- Until taken to the La Crosse poor farm a short time ago, Otto Bailey (or Boelle), age 62, had not had a bath since he was a small child. In the history of La Crosse County this was the worst case ever called to the attention of local authorities. The experience the attendants at the poor farm had in regard to removing the accumulation of 60 years of filth from Bailey's body is best left untold.

Suffice it to say the old man was nearly scared to death. A short time after his bath he told a visiting friend that the poor farm was a place of horrors: that they were killing people there. Startled, the friend asked what he meant and the old man explained, "Why they make people here take a bath every week. I never had one before and don't believe I'll live long."

The poor farm once before had a case that was nearly as bad. It was that of an old man named Anderson, aged 80, who had not been immersed in water since 1862. When the attendants attempted to get him into the bath when he was taken to the

farm last summer he broke away and made his escape, coming back to town. Later he was returned to the farm and died after taking poison just before the poor commissioner came after him.

—*La Crosse Tribune*
March 24, 1906

Makes His Third Odd Trip
Milwaukee Man Again Claims Strange Home At Racine

MILWAUKEE- Frank Mosehetz, 581 Orchard Street, Milwaukee, is in the hands of the police. Some months ago, Mosehetz walked into the home of John Brown, agent of the Goodrich Transportation Company, and declared it was his property. The police took him in charge. His wife took him home. Not long after, he again walked into the Brown residence and proceeded to take possession and a second time his wife came and took him away. For the third time he arrived last night, walking all the way from Milwaukee. The strange part of the man's action is that he never lived in the city, was not a visitor here, is not known by Mr. and Mrs. Brown, in fact they never saw or heard of him in their lives until he walked into the house.

—Eau Claire Leader
August 4, 1906

❖ ❖ ❖

Saves Teeth Of The Dead
Janesville Woman Has Husband's False Molars Fitted To Her Own Mouth

FORT ATKINSON- Mrs. August Kramer, a thrifty little German woman of sixty summers, who resides near Fort Atkinson, should make her way in the world if true economy burns out. Twenty years ago Dr. A.P. Burros of Janesville made a false set of teeth for her husband consisting of upper and lower plates. For eighteen years these teeth served all purposes and would undoubtedly have lasted fifty years had not Mr. Kramer died two years ago. Just prior to placing the body in the casket, Mrs. Kramer asked that her husband's false teeth be removed, as she would soon be obliged to purchase a set. Her request was compiled with and Mrs. Kramer arrived in Janesville last week with her husband's full set of plates. She called upon Dr. Burros informing him that she desired to have them remade to fit her,

and the request was soon granted. When the little women of sixty years left the dental office she hoped that the teeth would make her thirty years younger as she intended soon again enter the matrimonial class.

—Eau Claire Leader
May 21, 1907

❖ ❖ ❖

Penninsula "Wild Man" Caught

EAU CLAIRE- The "wild" man, who has been wandering in the vicinity of Misesauno Island, and who is reported to have been killing cattle and cutting out their hearts, was brought to the county jail yesterday. His name is John Phillips. He claims that his home is in New Buffalo, Mich., but others say that he comes from Stephenson, in Menominee County. He was found wandering in the woods by Deputy Sheriff Cota and offered resistance.

—Eau Claire Leader
May 21, 1907

❖ ❖ ❖

He Barks Like Dog
Milwaukee Physicians Are Puzzled Over Mysterious Malady Of Joseph Volk. Not Hydrophobia.

MILWAUKEE- The mysterious malady of Joseph Volk, 928 Locust St., is puzzling Milwaukee Physicians.

WRECK NEAR LYNDHURST WIS.

Volk is at time seized with an irresistible impulse to bark like a dog. In other respects he appears to be rational. He told the doctors that he barked for the mental pleasure it afforded him.

"He said last night that he could stop if he wanted to, and promised to refrain in the future. But this morning he had another barking spell," said Dr. McKinley at Emergency hospital. "It more resembles the peculiar bark of a sea lion than it does the bark of a dog. It isn't hydrophobia. I don't know what it is."

—*Milwaukee Journal*
February 12, 1908

Barefooted Man

WINTER- A letter from one of the Kaiser Lumber Co.'s camps near Winter, in which some Chippewa people are employed, states that the crew was startled upon arising Monday morning to see the snow tramped down by bare feet. Both feet of the man were plainly seen in the snow. The tracks came from the north, circled around the sleeping shanty several times, paced back and forth to the barn and finally disappeared in a westerly direction. The boys are curious to learn who made the tracks why they were made by bare feet and are unable to solve the mystery. Not only were the feet shoeless, but stocking-less.

—*Eau Claire Leader*
January 7, 1908

"This building which was built in 1905 is the former office of the Kaiser Lumber Company. It is one of the few remaining buildings from Eau Claire's great lumber industry which got its start in the 1860s. Kaiser Lumber Company was formed in 1905 by John Kaiser and employed 350 persons at its peak. It closed in 1939 bringing an end to the Eau Claire lumber industry."

From the sign in front of the Kaiser Lumber Company Historic Building in Eau Claire.

Woman Cured Through Prayer

**Mrs. Lydia Piatt,
An Invalid For Twenty Years,
Suddenly Becomes Well.
Physicians Had All Told Her That
She Would Never Be Better.
She Attributes Her Restoration To
God In Answer To Her Prayers.**

FOND DU LAC- The most remarkable cure ever witnessed in this city, and indeed one of the strangest ever known in Wisconsin, has just occurred and it will never constitute an advertisement for any medicine nostrum. After twenty years of constant suffering, during the greater part of which time she was unable to get about except by means of crutches and the assistance of others, Mrs. Lydia Piatt suddenly arose from her bed and after walking about the room for a few moments went down stairs and nearly frightened the matron into hysterics by her sudden transformation from a decrepit invalid into a healthy, sprightly woman, whose step was as elastic as one who had known neither sickness nor lameness.

It was Friday the 13th, and by no means an unlucky day so far as Mrs. Piatt was concerned, for she continued going about the house and assisting the matron and the nurses in the several rounds of duties. The shock once over, the news seemed too good to be true and for that reason no publicity was given the event at the time. However, the following day, Saturday, Mrs. Piatt insisted on paying a visit to her mother for the first time in several years and not only went, but walked the entire distance, there and back, nearly three miles in all. Every one was astonished and still more so on Sunday morning when she showed no signs of fatigue and announced her intention of attending church, a privilege she had been compelled to forego for many years. She is a member of the Division Street Methodist Church, and attended services, startling her old friends almost as much as one risen from the dead.

—*Milwaukee Journal*
January 17, 1899

In 1900, 42% of the workforce was in farming.

Case Of Divine Healing

**James Hodge Cured Of Pneumonia
By President Croft Of
Mormon Church**

WAUCOUSTA- The town of Waucousta, this county, is to the front with what is claimed to be a case of divine healing. James Hodge, an old resident and a member of the Mormon Church, was very ill of pneumonia and grew rapidly worse. President Croft of the Wisconsin conference was summoned and it is said that as soon as he had ministered to the man's wants, the pain disappeared and the patient instantly recovered.

—*Milwaukee Journal*
January 20, 1899

CHAPTER 7 PSYCHIC PHENOMENA

Her Broken Neck
Cured By Prayer

OSHKOSH- Valentina Costa, who came to St. Mary's Hospital with a broken neck, has been cured, as she believes as a direct result of prayer. Her family lives in Green Bay. The little girl is deeply religious and has prayed earnestly for recovery. Thursday night, while on her knees in the chapel of the hospital, the brace to her head broke, and instead of wobbling about as formerly, the girl was overjoyed to discover that the head remained erect and in position and that she could turn it from side to side.

—*Milwaukee Journal*
February 12, 1900

Strange
Psychic Phenomena
Which Puzzles
Waukesha Family

WAUKESHA- People who are interested in the study of psychic phenomena will be interested in an occurrence which took place in a prominent Waukesha family a few days ago. The head of the family is a prominent lawyer well known in more states than Wisconsin. The family consists of the lawyer, his wife and a daughter about 10 years old. The little girl is a bright little thing, but has never given any indication that she was any different from the ordinary child of her age.

The little girl's grandmother has been lying with the family this winter. Tuesday, while the girl was at school, the grandmother went to another part of the city where she had some property and she had not returned when her granddaughter came home from school. When the child came home she went upstairs to lay off her wraps and came down again in a few moments. The mother said, "I wonder whether grandma will come home to dinner?"

"Why she's home," said the child. "I just met her on the stairs as I was coming down." "That's queer," said the mother, "I should have thought she would have taken her things downstairs." Dinner was ready in a few moments and the mother told the child to call her grandmother. The little one ran upstairs and in a moment called down to her mother that she couldn't find her grandmother. The mother went upstairs, but no one was found. She said the child had been mistaken, but the little one insisted that she saw her grandmother. She said that the old lady was on the fourth step from the top and said "hello" to her as they passed. She then described what her grandmother wore and particularly a scarf which she had never seen her wear before. The mother was still skeptical.

After dinner the child returned to school and in the afternoon the grandmother came home. She had on the identical scarf that the child had described and was dressed in every particular as the child she said she was, but she declares positively that she was not at home at noon. The little girl still insists that she saw her grandma on the stairs. The question is, what did she see?

—*Milwaukee Journal*
March 17, 1900

❖ ❖ ❖

Study Drives Him Insane

JANESVILLE- A.J. Dayton of this city has become insane, it is believed, from constant study in trying to invent a perpetual motion machine.

—*Milwaukee Journal*
April 6, 1900

❖ ❖ ❖

Hypnotized Into Marriage

INDIAN FORD- Ethel Heath, 14 years old, asserted in court that she was hypnotized into leaving her home in Indian Ford County, Wis., by Chas Laclair, who was under arrest on a charge of abducting her. W.F. Heath, her father, after the girl had sent for him, had Laclair arrested, charging him with abduction. Laclair admitted his quilt after the girl had testified.

—*Milwaukee Journal*
June 18, 1900

❖ ❖ ❖

His Dreams Came True
La Crosse Farmer Has Vision Of Riches And They Are His

LA CROSSE- John Brienner, a farmer residing a few miles south of here, dreamed of a fortune for himself, and the dream came true, after it had been repeated the proverbial three times. Mr. Brienner is a native of Germany and came to America forty years ago, while yet a child. In relating the story, Mr. Brienner said that he was too young to note or remember the circumstances on his voyage of his former home. He knew nothing of his antecedents until recently, when in his dreams a voice spoke strange words in his ear, and he arose and wrote them down. He knew no Latin, but the writing was always in that dead language, perfect in every respect. When translated, it told him many things. His first wife had died a few years ago, when he resided in Chicago, and one revelation, which has since been proven to be true, was that of her grave, long neglected, had been visited and beautified by an unknown hand.

Mr. Brienner said that the most important information found in the letters in Latin was of Germany. In the home of his ancestors, said the strange language, there is a large tract of land. It belongs to John Brienner, who was taken away from his parents in early infancy, probably for the purpose of diverting the prospective heir. The strange dreams so wrought up the farmer that he wrote to his friends in Germany. Reply came back that the land was there, a fortune of no small magnitude to the successful claimant, and he has only to establish his identity in order to assert his title. He is now arranging to sell or rent his farm near this city, in order that he may make a trip to Germany and secure the heritage of which he has been deprived these many years.

—*Milwaukee Journal*
December 8, 1900

Medium At Fond Du Lac Predicts Three Big Fires

FOND DU LAC- Policeman will closely watch three principal buildings of this city as the result of the prophecy of a Spiritualistic medium who says this city is to be visited by three costly fires within the next three months. The medium has given the owners and occupants of the three doomed buildings warning of the impending disaster and advised them to insure heavily.

—*Milwaukee Journal*
April 30, 1902

Spiritualism Figures In Many Divorce Cases
Information Received In Séances Causes Many Family Quarrels With Serious Results

MILWAUKEE- Attorneys say that there has been a noticeable recurrence lately of divorce proceedings in which the cause of marital disagreement has been due to the work of alleged spiritualistic mediums. It is the practice, particularly in the northwestern part of the city, among the German-Americans, for the women to hold afternoon gatherings, usually ostensibly kaffee-klatches, in which a medium is generally present and experiments in spiritualistic phenomena are the main diversions.

So absorbed in the practice do the women become that they govern themselves in accordance with the spiritual advice received and domestic discord of times result. Judge Ludwig's court has been the theatre of a divorce proceeding of the sort indicated, and for three days the spectators' seats have been crowded with housewives from what used to be called the "wooden shoe district" of the North Side, most of whom were witnesses. The suit for divorce was brought by Fred Mau, a grocer at Buffum and Hadley Streets, who alleged that, as a results of neighborhood séances, his wife, Elizabeth Mau, had become abusive toward him and suspicious as to the intentions towards her. She imagined that he had designs on her life and frequently called him a "Luetgert" and similar suggestive names. He claimed that she had had spiritual information that he had but a year to live and that she was planning as to use to be made of his life insurance of $2,000. On her part Mrs. Mau claimed that her husband was cruel to her, and the family appears to have split even in the matter, as one of the grown-up sons sat with the father in court while the other occupied a seat beside the mother. A well-known attorney who was present during a part of the trial said that he personally knew of twelve recent divorce cases in which the spiritualistic feature figured.

—*Milwaukee Journal*
February 2, 1901

❖ ❖ ❖

Foretold By Dream
Appleton Girl Has Leg Fractured After Seeing Vision Of It

APPLETON- Theresa, the daughter of Joseph Gruelich fell from a fence and fractured her leg. The previous night the little girl dreamed she fractured her leg and a few hours before the accident occurred informed her mother of the fact.

—*Milwaukee Journal*
October 1, 1901

❖ ❖ ❖

Money Found In Answer To Prayer

RACINE- The valuable package lost from the American Express office several weeks ago was found as an answer to prayer, says the young man who last handled the package. His sister had prayed for the delivery of the parcel. She told her brother that her prayers had been answered and that he

would find the package when he entered the office. Her prophecy came true and the young man believes that the package was placed in that drawer by the power of prayer.

—*Milwaukee Journal*
December 26, 1901

Modern Miracles
Cures Performed Last Night That Rival Those Of 1500 Years Ago

JANESVILLE- "Wonderful!" "Astonishing," "Marvelous!" "The work of God," "Miraculous!" "How can he do it?" and many like expressions were heard as the throng surged out of the Opera House last night, after witnessing the most interesting exhibition of healing the sick ever performed in this part of the country.

CHAPTER 7 PSYCHIC PHENOMENA

There has never been a medical practitioner or any other man in this city who attracted so much attention or been the object of such great praise as has been accorded this youthful healer since his advent here. He is the talk of the town. One hears and sees nothing but "Boy Phenomenon." He is the chief topic of conversation on the streets, in the stores, on the cars, in the offices, at home, in fact, everywhere. His name, coupled with the marvelous cures he accomplished last night in the stage before hundreds of representative citizens of Janesville has created an exciting episode in our city.

There were many of our most prominent and intellectual citizens in the audience, including leading physicians, lawyers and judges and businessmen. As usual many were, no doubt, very skeptical when they went in, but all of one mind as they went out, and that was the magnetism possessed by the "Boy Phenomenon," undoubtedly possessing wonderful healing qualities. Tonight will occur the second and last public exhibition. Those who are interested in the work, and all who are on crutches and canes, the lame, deaf and sick who wish to be cured will be given front seats and treated free upon the stage. Admission free to all adults.

About a half dozen wellknown citizens were treated last night suffering from as many different diseases, and by his wonderful life-giving magnetism restored paralyzed limbs to usefulness, made the deaf hear, the blind to see and the lame to walk. In each instance, the patient demonstrated by their actions and testified by words the great benefits derived. While there were many remarkable cures performed, time prevents a more extended notice in this article. Suffice to say, he did all and more than his advertisement claimed for him. Those who desire private treatment and are able to pay a small price to be treated may call at the Hotel Myers any time during the next two weeks, and receive consultation, examination and a thorough diagnosia at which time the examining physicians will decide if your case is curable, and if so, the price of the treatment will be named. No free cases treated at the hotel. Those wishing for treatment must go to the Opera House tonight. Office hours 10 a.m. to 5 p.m., daily except the Sabbath.

—*Janesville Daily Gazette*
March 5, 1902

In 1890, the average annual income for a family of four was $380.

Wife's Voice Returns
Result Of Dying Wish

BELOIT- The husband of Mrs. Philo M. Pierce lying at the point of death, expressed the wish that he might hear her voice again. She had been deprived of speech for three months. Within half an hour she began to talk to him and her voice seemed completely restored. Mr. Pierce, one of Beloit's pioneers and wealthiest citizens, died last night, aged 84.

—*Milwaukee Journal*
May 5, 1902

HIDDEN HEADLINES of WISCONSIN

Find Human Skull As Result Of Hypnotism

PRAIRIE DU CHIEN- Dr. McAee, a hypnotist, who has been giving exhibitions here the past week, put a young man named Bitterdee in a hypnotic state with a view of ascertaining where his father, who has been missing for over four years, was. The lad, while in this state, said that his father had been hit in the back of the head and killed, and the body buried at a certain place. While excavations were being made at the place signified a skull of a human being was unearthed. Doctors who examined the skull say it is genuine.

—*Milwaukee Journal*
July 14, 1902

❖ ❖ ❖

Mystery In A Skull
Boy Under Hypnotic Spell Names Spot Where Found

PRAIRIE DU CHIEN- Intense excitement prevailed here last night over the finding of the skull of a man under a pile if refuse. Dr. McAee, a hypnotist, has been giving exhibitions here the past week, and yesterday afternoon put a young man by the name of Bitterdee in a hypnotic state with a view of ascertaining where his father was. The latter has been missing for over four years. The lad, while in the state, said that his father had been hit in the back of the head and killed and the body buried at the place above stated.

An examination of the place was made last night and while excavations were being made a skull of a human being was unearthed. Doctors who examined the skull say it is genuine. Further investigations will be made tomorrow, which will probably throw more light in the mysterious discovery.

—*Eau Claire Weekly Telegram*
July 17, 1902

❖ ❖ ❖

Hypnotized By Indian
Is Found In A Stupor

ASHLAND- Ida Franz, aged 16, who was found in an Indian's shack on the Odanah reservation near Ashland, says that she was under the spell of a peculiar hypnotic influence, exercised by Thomas Beeson, the Indian with whom she left this city. Attorney Fred Hartwell, who rescued her found her, it was said, in a stupefied condition. After her rescue, a band of Indians started out to capture her again, but were beaten into Ashland, and gave up the chase. Attorney Hartwell says he can find no record of the girl's reported marriage to Beeson.

—*Milwaukee Journal*
October 6, 1902

❖ ❖ ❖

Palmistry
Some Remarkable Readings By MME. Budda

EAU CLAIRE- The Leader has heard of several wonderful demonstrations of the ability of Mme. Budda, who is stopping at No. 316 Eau Claire Street, opposite Eau

Claire House and which offered unquestioned evidence that Mme. Budda is a gifted clairvoyant and palmist. Her visitors include many well known citizens, all of whom express satisfaction that the readings are fair and honest.

A Chippewa resident who visited this gifted medium and palmist struck the key note when he first remarked that "My past and present were called so closely as to make me wonder if Mme. Budda had not by some manner come into possession of a diary kept by me, which of course was not the case, but her predictions and revelations are simply marvelous." She is well worthy of Eau Claire's patronage.

—*Eau Claire Leader*
June 2, 1904

❖ ❖ ❖

Hypnotism At Chetek

A Man Pitches Hay
Without Tines.
It Must Be True,
As The Alert Has It Down Fine.

CHETEK- A peculiar accident happened to J.M. Foster while haying one day last week. The cows got into his corn during the pitching operations and Mr. Foster ran straight away fork in hand to drive them out. On the way back, he sat down under a tree to rest for a minute and if possible to regain his atmospheric equilibrium. Before the flicker of a moment J.M. was fast asleep, snoring from one lake shore to the other. A fisherman or game warden heard the awful noise and ran to his relief. Mistaking the fork for a spear, the warden removed the prongs, leaving only the handle in Mr. Foster's possession.

When the haymaker awoke, Old Sol was still glimmering in the western sky, but showed signs of getting ready to don his nightcap. Without delay J.M. ran back to the hay field to again attack the fragrant hay-cocks. One after another they rose until the monster hay wagon was oiled high with the timothy and clover. Just then J.P. Lees happened around on his side. "Why what's become of your fork?" "My fork and I have been pitching here for two hours."

—*Eau Claire Leader*
August 2, 1905

❖ ❖ ❖

Spook Union Is Formed
Wisconsin Mediums File Articles
For A Protective Association

MADISON- The trust germ has invaded even the realm of ghosts. There was incorporated at Madison the Mediums' Protective Association. The incorporators propose to issue the mediums a working card, which will authorize them to interview spirits and receive and transmit messages so long as they live up to the rules of the association. At present the association is limited to fourteen members, all but two of whom reside in this city. Those applying for admission will be examined by members. It is explained that this course has become necessary owing to the number of "fake" mediums.

—*Eau Claire Leader*
November 24, 1905

Spiritualists Hold Meeting
Will R. Erwood Discusses Subject Last Night

EAU CLAIRE- Last evening about fifty persons gathered at Chappell Hall to listen to Will R. Erwood lecture upon spiritualism. He chose as his subject, "Spiritualism, God and the Bible." In opening the meeting Mr. Erwood stated that in place of the customary invocation he would read a poem by Ella Wheller Wilcox, "God and Me," which he read in a masterful manner. He then started in upon his subject, which dealt altogether with life after death, and in which he told of numerous instances where the spirits of those departed had returned and made themselves manifest in different ways by rappings, writing upon slates, etc., and stated it as his belief that the transition of the body known to most of us as death was merely a change from the material to the spiritual life. Mr. Erwood said that, while a great many persons were under the impression that only persons of inferior intellect or weak minds were believers in spiritualism—on the contrary, the sect numbered among its believers some of the greatest thinkers of the present day, and named many of them. Following his lecture, Mrs. Amanda Coffman, the noted test medium, gave an illustration of communication with the departed. It was certainly very interesting and while undoubtedly many differ as to beliefs, there should have been a larger attendance.

—*Eau Claire Leader*
April 11, 1906

Intended Bride Hypnotized
Friends Of Kenosha Girl Attempting To Prevent Marriage

KENOSHA- The friends of Miss Marie Watson, of this city (Kenosha), are making every possible effort to prevent her marriage to William Jackson, a bartender employed at the Powers Lake Hotel in this county. Judge Slosson of Kenosha County Court, and Justice Sturgess of the city, yesterday refused to marry the couple and both declared that in their opinion the girl was under hypnotic spell. The couple left Powers Lake, stating that they were going to Indiana to get married.

—*Eau Claire Leader*
August 2, 1906

❖ ❖ ❖

Medium Gives Clue
Brother Mourned Eleven Years As Dead Found To Be Alive

EAU CLAIRE- Through a trance medium and the government authorities, acting upon the clue of the former, Charles J. Chalsma of this city has located William Kniggie a brother-in-law, who has been mourned as dead for eleven years. William Kniggie is a resident of Brownsville, Minn., and disappeared in 1895, leaving his wife and children. He corresponded for some time, then all trace of him was lost.

Charles Chalsma, brother of his wife, a short time ago visited a trance medium and was informed that the missing man was

"straight west of here, and that he is marching now with a regiment of soldiers, for I can hear his legs rubbing." On this almost groundless hope, Mr. Chalsma wrote to the war department and in reply was informed that William Kniggie, this missing man, was a member of Company C. Nineteenth U.S. Infantry, on duty at Camp Tayabes, Philippine Islands. The official information declares further that he was in good standing and in good health on June 30.

—*Eau Claire Leader*
July 18, 1906

Puts Woman In Trance To Exorcise Spirit

MILWAUKEE- Milwaukee Spiritualists, who attended the picnic of the society yesterday in the grove south of the city were told by Mrs. B.M. Rageth, 618 Russell Avenue, who renounced Catholicism to become a medium that they need no priests or ministers. She placed Mrs. William Tede, 471 American Avenue, in a trance to drive away an evil spirit. When she snapped her fingers and awakened Mrs. Tede the medium said, she had succeeded.

Mrs. Rageth said her spirit control is a Catholic priest. Ald. Henry Smith told of his conversation from the Presbyterian faith to Spiritualism. He said he went out into the woods and the birds taught him the new belief. His work as an alderman had been guided by a good spirit. Ald. Smith predicts that within two years people on earth will be able to communicate with the nearer planets by wireless telegraph.

—*Eau Claire Leader*
July 17, 1907

❖ ❖ ❖

Fortune Telling Is A Luxury

EAU CLAIRE- A palmist, who is holding forth at a hotel in Chippewa Falls, yesterday came to Eau Claire for the purpose of opening a parlor for "readings" in the city. She visited police headquarters during the early morning to enquire about the license charged for such vocations in the city. The police officers were not sure what the license was, as few palmists have considered Eau Claire a fertile field for the reading of palms. Mayor Frawley was still dreaming at that early hour and city Clerk Fennessey was just eating his morning meal. The woman was disappointed. Later in the day she obtained the desired information. When informed that the license was only $10 a day, she nearly fainted. It is not known whether she will come down from Chippewa or not.

—*Eau Claire Leader*
August 24, 1907

Clairvoyant Hopes To Find Missing Man

EAU CLAIRE- Prof. Roberts, the Milwaukee man clairvoyant, arrived today and went to Cedar River, Mich. to locate Frank Hayward who has been missing since June 8. He disappeared at that time from a lumber camp and has not been seen or heard from since. His brother, a wealthy New York attorney, is making strenuous efforts to find him and Roberts on that account was summoned. Roberts claims to have foretold the finding of the body of Duncan McGregor, the Peshtigo lumberman who has been missing for months and whose remains were finally recovered in the river nearby.

—*Eau Claire Leader*
August 13, 1907

❖ ❖ ❖

Palmistry In Chippewa Falls
Leader Representative Visits Palmister And Undergoes Interesting Operation.
Terrible Predictions For The Scribe, But He Manages To Escape With Some Money.

CHIPPEWA FALLS- As the gilded youth is wont to remark, I "just positively dote" on palmisters. I don't mean by this remark that I am in love with any of them, for some palmisters are married and other wouldn't be a 10 to 1 shot in the leather medal contest at the beauty show. But when I see a palmister's sign I just can't resist the temptation to be palmed immediately. While strolling about Chippewa Falls yesterday afternoon I noticed such a sign on the door of a residence and I dropped in. Dropped is almost the appropriate word. I intended to walk in, but just as I was about to open the door some one from the inside opened it and I fell in. The sign remained outside. I felt as embarrassed as a Chicago mounted cop and doubtless appeared as awkward. When I recovered my breath and recuperated my dignity I was ushered into the inner sanctum and seated.

When you desire to be palmed it is considered a breach of etiquette not to wash your hands before undergoing the trying ordeal. No refined palmister desires to hold hands with you and murmur sweet nothings in your ear, at so much per, when those same hands would imply that you were the king pin of the fraternity of hoboes. To continue this outpouring of a troubled soul, the palmist requested that I cross her hand with a silver dollar. A lead dollar is better suited for this purpose, should you be fortunate enough to have any in your clothes. As I crossed her palm with the silver piece it closed as unexpectedly as do some of the Chicago banks. A thrill of joy like that experienced by the mother who fails to cop the prize at the baby show shot through my dilating bosom and I heaved a pair of useless sighs. My dollar was gone. She had palmed it. I still remained to be palmed. With a Cassie Chadwick smile she grasped my left hand firmly. Her grip brought back vivid recollections of the Democratic presidential campaign congratulations which are now recorded in ancient history. She held my hand until the fear passed—fortunately there was no traction congestion at

the time——carefully scrutinizing the lines of my palm, which I am loath to admit resemble one of the terminals of the Vanderbilt four-track system. With a dreamy, far-away look in her dark brown orbs, she quietly remarked that I was a poet. Before she had time to reverse the decision I passed out another dollar. I had never before been accused of such a thing and my whole being thrilled with the same variety of ecstasy that crops out in a soul of the innocent bystander who hears the harmonious notes of an auto horn about three feet in his rear.

You will wed an heiress, the palmist continued. I thanked her for the information but heiresses come high. I had donated another dollar to the cause of science when she went into the trance. The next time I go to a palmist's I'll endeavor to marry a biscuit shooter or a chamber janitor and ask her the benefit of the special rate. "You have experienced much trouble," the palmist said. I deny the allegation. I have never been married, never mixed in politics and never owned an auto. My life has been one sweet dream of bliss. "You are bound to rise in the world." So is the aeronaut, the elevator boy and the man who fools with dynamite. "You will live to be sixty." And then an orderly vigilance committee will quietly string me up to the nearest trolley pole for inflicting such dope as this on an unsuspecting and altogether too patient public. "You will marry for a second time." I reached for my pocketbook, but she continued her predictions and a I got a cheap wife as a result. "You will be the father of twenty-three children." And then somebody will hand me a lemon. Will certainly need an heiress, even though the stereotyped autographed letter of congratulation from "Teddy" should be forthcoming. "You will reside in a warmer climate at some future date." Delightfully encouraging, but what newspaper scribe can hope for anything better. "You have recently completed a long journey." That was the day I walked in from Badger Mills. "You make no effort to save your money." What's the use? The palmisters would have to cease business if we all saved our coin. "You—" But the doorbell rang at the critical moment. This was my cue that the séance was terminated. Another easy mark, with a hankering to be separated from his shekels, was ushered into the room. I cast a lingering, pitying glance at the intended victim, and then walked out into the cold, materialistic world. Truly, it is great to be palmed.

—Eau Claire Leader
September 11, 1907

❖ ❖ ❖

She Foretold
Engineer On Central Receives A Strange Warning

OSHKOSH- Horace Warner, the Wisconsin Central Engineer who was killed in the wreck at Oshkosh, was foretold of his death last summer by Miss Lottie Holmes, a Hindoo who warned him that unless he quit the railroad he would be killed in a collision within a year. By his death the entire Warner family has passed away. Mr. Warner's father died a year ago at Steven's Point and four weeks later his mother passed away and only a month ago his sister died. Mr. Warner was engaged to

marry Miss Marie Doercher of Neenah in March. He was a member of Company 1 of that city and resided there for a long time before coming to the village.

—Eau Claire Leader
February 6, 1909

❖ ❖ ❖

Cured As By A Miracle

SOLON SPRINGS- Neelie Carolyn Nicholls, an 18-year-old girl at Salon Springs, in this county, is able to sit up, after she had been compelled to lie on her back for six years. She sat up last night and took supper with her folks for the first time since she became sick. The cure is claimed to have been effected by one Sherman, a divine healer from Brockville, Ont., in two days. The girl's feet were twisted out of shape, as was her backbone. He worked these with his hands and in a very few minutes they began to take on their natural form. Excitement runs high over the affair and the people are pouring into Solon Springs.

—Eau Claire Leader
August 26 1907

❖ ❖ ❖

A Creepy Experience

GRAND RAPIDS- The Rev. Clarence Godfrey, on retiring one night, determined that he would try to "telepath" a phantasm of himself to a lady living in another part of the city, tells H. Addington Bruco in *Success Magazine.* For about ten minutes he endeavored in thought to appear to her. At the end of that time he fell asleep.

About four hours later the lady on whom he had been "exerting his will" awoke with an impression that she had heard a curious sound. She felt nervous and uneasy and thought that if she went downstairs and tool a drink of soda water it might have a quieting effect. Coming back she was astounded to see the form of Mr. Godfrey standing on the staircase. He remained standing there for three or four seconds, while she stared at him in horrified amazement. Then, as she approached the staircase, he disappeared.

—*The Grand Rapids Tribune*
August 17, 1910

❖❖❖

Was Converted As A Spook

Though A Scoffer In Life, Spiritualist Declares Dr. W.D. Thompson, A Noted Wisconsin Divine Now Dead, Has Sent Several Messages To Mortals On This Earth

WONEWOC- Claiming the conversion of an unbeliever to the cause of spiritualism since death, Spiritualists encamped at Wonewoc have startled and shocked friends of the late Rev. W.D. Thomas, of this city, who died suddenly on a train near Camp Douglas a few months ago. Dr. Thomas, who was one of the best known and most prominent Episcopal divines in the Northwest, was not a believer in spiritualism. After careful research he had cast aside the theories of the spiritualists. G. Bodmenr, writing to W.R. Trumbull, of this city, describing the séance at which Dr. Thomas' spirit is alleged to have appeared,

says, "First came Tom Lafferty, imitating an engine coming from afar. He spoke to four of us. He was killed in a collision. Then came my grandmother, talking plain German to me. Next came in a loud voice, Rev. Thomas. I asked, "Is this the Rev. Thomas from La Crosse?" Answer: "Yes, yes." I asked, "What do you think of spiritualism now?" Answer: "Oh, it's all true, it's all true: I was blind before I crossed the river, I will come to talk."

While friends of Dr. Thomas demand identification of the spirit before they will accept the truth of the spiritualist's claim, they admit that the rapid repetition of words such as "yes, yes" and "it's all true, it's all true" is decidedly characteristic of the doctor. The expression "I am blind" is also quoted as being characteristic of the doctor whose eccentricities of expression and speech, in life, were peculiar.

—*Eau Claire Leader*
July 16, 1909

HIDDEN HEADLINES of WISCONSIN

Nature's Sky Painting

JANESVILLE- Last evening, just after dark, a narrow band of luminous vapor was noticed stretched across the sky from the eastern to the western horizon and about ten degrees south of the zenith. This was visible about half an hour, and shortly after its disappearance a brilliant aurora lighted up the northern sky, continuing several hours. The night was clear and starlit and the phenomenon exhibited itself to an excellent advantage.

—*Janesville Gazette*
November 11, 1871

❖ ❖ ❖

An Unusual Phenomenon

JANESVILLE- An unusual phenomenon occurred on last Tuesday evening. After the very sudden and unlooked for shower of rain, which fell while the moon was shining brightly, there appeared at the north of the city a beautiful bright, white rainbow, or, as some term it, a moonbow. This is an unheard of occurrence to "the oldest inhabitant."

—*Janesville Gazette*
August 25, 1877

❖ ❖ ❖

Meteoric

FOND DU LAC- At 2 o'clock this morning a brilliant meteor of a bluish-red color, apparently about six feet in diameter, burst over the south part of the city. It was wit-

nessed by the Fire Department which was operating close by. Some who saw it thought the world was on fire, and were much frightened.

—*Janesville Gazette*
January 29, 1879

❖ ❖ ❖

Bright Meteor

WAUKESHA- A very bright meteor was seen in the eastern sky at Waukesha last evening. It gave forth a blue light and as an attractive sight.

—*Waukesha Freeman*
January 4, 1883

❖ ❖ ❖

Strange Appearance

OSHKOSH- There was a very strange appearance in the heavens last night in the shape of a pink band that extended through the moon to the east and west horizon, apparently exactly marking the moon's path. There were no evidence of the borealis in the north, and this phenomenon was the only strange one visible overhead.

—*Oshkosh Daily Northwestern*
October 17, 1883

❖ ❖ ❖

An Unusual Sight
Mirage Witnessed By A Number Of Green Bay People

GREEN BAY- Joseph Nick, George Sienger and many other well-known and reputable citizens are discussing a peculiar spectacle they witnessed last evening in the eastern sky. It is described as a ball of fire about ten feet in diameter and perfectly round. The color was dark red and the object hung far above the horizon, disappearing in about ten minutes after first being seen.

Later in the evening the moon rose in the same quarter, and some of them who saw the strange spectacle are inclined to regard it as a mirage in which the yet invisible orb of night was in some way magnified and reflected on the sky.

—Centralia Enterprise and Tribune
December 14, 1895

❖ ❖ ❖

Bright Light

MARSHFIELD- A very bright light was discovered in the northwest Monday morning at three o'clock.

—Marshfield Times and Gazette
April 18, 1885

❖ ❖ ❖

Great Ball Of Fire

SOMERS- A great ball of fire appeared in the eastern sky on Sunday evening, supposed to be the explosion of a meteor and was accompanied by a rumbling noise as of distant thunder.

—Racine Weekly Journal
November 28, 1895

Scared By Meteor
Hot Rock Falls With Great Force, Apparently From The Sky

MARINETTE- The falling last night of meteorite or volcanic rock, apparently from the sky, startled two Marinette men. The rock fell with great force, was hot, and shows fire. In composition it does not correspond with geological formations.

—Milwaukee Journal
June 10, 1902

❖ ❖ ❖

Mysterious Thing In The Sky
Appleton People Saw A Floating Object And Think It Was An Airship

APPLETON- Perhaps 100 people who happened to be on the West College Avenue at 7:30 o'clock the other evening claim to have seen an object which was not a cloud nor a balloon or anything of the sort, pass over the city with great rapidity. Its distance from the earth was too great to permit of any attempt at description, but many thought it was an airship.

—Eau Claire Weekly
July 30, 1903

Fairy Story From La Crosse

GENOA- Harry Clements, foreman of the Genoa (Wis.) pearl factory, Charles Warne and a dozen other residents of the village assert positively that two large cigar-shaped airships passed over that village at a high elevation the other afternoon. According to the story of the men, the machines were supported by balloons and were propelled by huge wheels which made a buzzing sound. The ships were pointed northward and were traveling slowly. The story is declared to be true by some of the most reliable residents of Genoa.

—*Eau Claire Weekly Telegram*
October 8, 1903

> **In Wisconsin, the cities of Belleville, Dundee, and Elmwood all claim to be the "UFO Capital of the World."**

Meteor Strikes Near The City
**Farmer Named Smith Almost Overcome By The Gas.
Was So Thick No One Could See Their Hands Before Their Faces For Some Hours.
A Strange Phenomenon.**

JANESVILLE- Nearly suffocated by the fumes of gas, with his wife, and their three children hysterical with fear, Mr. Smith, a farmer near the blind institute, awakened the residents of J.O. Selleck's household on Center Avenue last evening and told them a story of having encountered a wave of gaseous matter a few rods away that had almost overcome him and his family. The children were crying and fearful and Mrs. Smith was equally fearful, so that the party was taken into the Selleck home while Mr. Selleck, George Clark, his son, and Mr. Smith drove back to the scene to discover the cause of the trouble.

The story Mr. Smith tells is of a wonderful sight and a still more wonderful phenomenon of nature. As he and his wife were driving home from the city at about half past nine they noticed a huge star-like light appear suddenly in the sky. It became brighter and brighter and suddenly seemed to swoop down and be swallowed up in the snowbanks that lined the road near the Blind Institute. As they turned onto the road after leaving the bridge the smell of a strange gas became so strong that Mr. Smith was nearly overcome and with difficulty was able to turn about and drive back to Mr. Selleck's.

When the party composed of Mr. Selleck, Mr. Clark, Mr. Miltimore and his son and Mr. Smith returned to the road where the smell had been the strongest, they were greeted by a dense fog-like substance which was so thick they could not see their hands in front of their faces, let alone the horse they were driving, which was but a few feet away.

This extended for several rods along the road and in places was even more dense than others. The smell was at times almost suffocating. It is described as resembling that of a gas retort or of the gas which escapes from the door of an open engine.

Although the gentleman remained in the vicinity of the supposed meteor for some hours they were unable to discover the meteor itself. This morning a party covered all the fields in the vicinity in a vain search and again this afternoon a large party is out trying to locate the meteor. According to Mr. Smith, just before the meteor struck the earth he heard a rushing sound like some huge body falling through the air and then came the blinding fog of noisome smell.

Professor Cornstock at the Washburn Observatory at Madison was called up by the Gazette office over the telephone at noon today, and asked regarding the phenomenon. He said, "It is undoubtedly a meteor. What caused the smell I can not say. That is some special condition of the soil in which it struck. Were it be in an oil or coal country it could easily be explained, but as I do not know the land about Janesville I can not state what it was. Under ordinary conditions the smell would have been that of a steam arising from a hot substance, like metal falling into a tub of water."

Prof. Cornstock is authority for all phenomena of the heavens and while he says that there is nothing strange in the falling of a meteor, he is surprised at the accompanying smell. Possibly this may develop an unknown coal field right in Janesville and possibly the meteor will be found to have contained a strange gaseous substance that was released when it struck the earth.

—*Janesville Daily Gazette*
February 20, 1904

Burned By
Hot Meteorite

LA CROSSE- After watching a flaming meteorite blaze through the sky and crash through three trees to hit the ground within a few feet of his doorstep, Frank Herlitzke, 803 Ferry Street, burned his hand severely while picking up the queer object. About 9:30 last night Mr. Herlitzke and his wife were sitting on the porch of their residence when some shinning object fell through nearby trees and landed in the boulevard in front of their house. Mr. Herlitzke, upon attempting to pick it up, found it to be red hot.

The object is described as being two inches long and of an irregular, rounded shape. It has all the appearances of a piece of coal but is much heavier, being metallic. It has been taken to the weather bureau where it will be examined.

—*La Crosse Tribune*
July 23, 1906

Meteor Strikes Eau Claire
Citizens Are Now Trying To Find
Where It Came From

EAU CLAIRE- Eau Claire was visited by a meteor about 11 o'clock Saturday night. Its visit was not announced and when it struck the ground in the vicinity of the Omaha yards it created no end of excitement. The meteor was witnessed by several people from the city, among them being Dr. Chase. Its flight through space somewhat resembled that of a big ball of fire which was as brilliant as an arc lamp. When the ball or meteor hit the earth it seemed to spread out and fly in all directions. It is reported to the Leader that the meteor is the same one that was noticed passing over the city of Madison Saturday evening. It is said that the spot where it fell is plainly visible, but no one as yet has found any portion of it, being burned so deep into the ground. A number of people visited the place yesterday and there were discussions galore as to where the meteor came from.

—*Eau Claire Leader*
April 21, 1908

Meteor Excited All Communities

One Which Fell In Eau Claire Was Seen In Many Cities. It Seemed To Pass Just Over The Tops Of The Buildings.

EAU CLAIRE- The meteor which fell on Eau Claire late last Saturday evening was seen earlier in the night passing over a number of Wisconsin cities. The awesome visitor created considerable excitement and no end of excitement. Dispatches to the Leader yesterday tell of the flight of the meteor. They are as follows: La Crosse, April 23. Communities in all directions from La Crosse are thoroughly stirred up over the visit of the big meteor, which in passing lighted Wisconsin and eastern Minnesota, as brightly, for a moment as the day. In La Crosse it seemed that the meteor passed directly over the city. It came from the northeast and passed swiftly to the southwest. From the earth its head appeared like a large round red ball about six feet in diameter, and the tail had the bright greenish white glare of sharp lightning and extended, seemingly for 150 to 200 feet behind it, dwindling into nothing. The meteor gave off sparks and "chunks" of light and resembled nothing so much as a huge sky-rocket.

Many people at first thought it was a great sky-rocket. A full minute and a half after it passed, there was a deep roar and in some places the ground was shaken as though by an earthquake. A heavy rumbling followed the first thunder, and the impression prevailed the meteor had struck somewhere near Brownsille. Reports from

Genoa, Brownsville, Caledonia, Houston and other surrounding towns shows that the meteor seemed as near to each of them as it did La Crosse, and no trace of it has been found yet. Whether it buried itself in the earth or exploded in the air is unknown.

—*Eau Claire Leader*
April 24, 1908

❖ ❖ ❖

Illuminated Light

RACINE- A bright light which illuminated the heavens in the northwest, at the time the storm was at its worst, leads people to believe that some barn or home was struck and catching fire, burned up.

—*Racine Daily Journal*
September 12, 1910

❖ ❖ ❖

Flaming Sword In The Sky

SARATOGA-   The people of lower Saratoga have been greatly excited the past week by what appears to be a flaming sword, apparently about three feet long with a beautiful jeweled handle, which has made its appearance in the heavens on several nights among the stars as seen from that locality. Some of the more superstitious of the inhabitants are firm in the conviction that this means war.

Whether it is war in the neighborhood or war on a world wide scale our informant sayeth not. But the God of war seems to have especially favored Saratoga in selecting the people of that town above all others to make known his intention to stir up bloody strife among men in the good, old sign language of the ancients. "Lay on MacDuff, and damned be he who first cries, hold, enough!"

—*Wisconsin Valley Leader*
December 17, 1908

Strange sightings in the sky still continue as each year UFOWisconsin.com receives over 100 reports from witnesses who have seen something unknown in Wisconsin's sky.

A Strange Phenomena
Luminous Display Similar To Northern Lights In Southeastern Skies

EAU CLAIRE- Our attention was called last evening to certain luminous phenomenon appearing not only in the northern sky, but also in the southeastern portion of the heavens. While the aurora borealis or northern lights are not uncommon, still we confess that we have never noticed before any such phenomenon in the southeastern sky. Scientists now agree that the aurora has an electrical origin and it is believed by some that the phenomenon is due to the passage of electrical currents through highly attenuated air at a considerable distance from the earth. The aurora sometimes continues a few hours, occasionally the night, and sometimes for several nights in succession. Periodicity in aurora displays has lately been asserted. A maximum occurs about once in ten years and a period of remarkable brilliancy about once in sixty years. We wish to thank Mrs. Sommersmeyer who so kindly called our attention to this extraordinary phenomenon of last evening.

—*Eau Claire Leader*
May 26, 1908

❖❖❖

Spiral Meteor

MILWAUKEE- Messrs. Rindskovy and Adler, students from Milwaukee, attending the State University, inform us that shortly after 9 o'clock last evening, they witnessed the fall of a large and brilliant meteor. It fell from near the zenith toward the southeast, and one peculiarity of its descent was that it came down spirally.

—*Wisconsin State Journal*
November 17, 1870

❖❖❖

Meteor Falls In Kenosha
Strange Ball Of Fire Descends, Burning Telephone Wires

KENOSHA- Darting and whirling through the air, a great ball of fire like a meteor descended on Kenosha yesterday morning, and striking a wire of the Kenosha Home Telephone company, burned the wire apart and put 200 telephones out of commission. Hundreds saw the ball of fire and declare it was 10 inches in circumference. It is supposed it was a meteor, but nothing could be found to show where it had buried itself in the ground. Men at the telephone board say it acted like a bolt of static lightning. It lighted up the entire heavens about the city.

—*Racine Journal*
August 30, 1910

INDEX
LISTED BY WISCONSIN TOWNS

HIDDEN HEADLINES of WISCONSIN

HIDDEN HEADLINES of WISCONSIN

HIDDEN HEADLINES of WISCONSIN

HIDDEN HEADLINES of WISCONSIN

PAGE 154

INDEX TOWNS

HIDDEN HEADLINES of WISCONSIN

HIDDEN HEADLINES of WISCONSIN

HIDDEN HEADLINES of WISCONSIN

.

About the Author

Chad Lewis is a paranormal investigator for Unexplained Research LLC, with a Master's Degree in Applied Psychology from the University of Wisconsin-Stout. Chad has spent years traveling the globe researching ghosts, strange creatures, crop formations, werewolves, and UFOs. Chad is a former State Director for the Mutual UFO Network and has worked with BLT Crop Circle Investigations. Chad is the organizer of *The Unexplained* Conferences and the host of *The Unexplained* paranormal radio talk show. He is the co-author of the *Road Guide to Haunted Locations* series.